Physicians' Guide
to the
Internet

ABOUT THE AUTHOR

Lee Hancock is an Educational Technologist with the University of Kansas Medical Center. By day, he writes and produces instructional videos or designs multimedia computer presentations to enhance classroom lectures. By night, he explores the Internet looking for anything that has to do with resources in health and medicine. Outside the university, Lee is best known for his Internet Health Sciences Resource List, which can be found throughout the Internet on various FTP sites and Gophers. Besides exploring the Internet, Lee writes and talks about Internet Health Resources. He has edited the *Key Guide to Electronic Resources: Health Sciences*, Information Today (was Learned Information, Inc.,) 1995, and has written for various newsletters about his Internet discoveries. In his spare time, Lee consults and gives workshops on the topic. Those presentations include Marion Merrill Dow, American Medical Informatics Association, Medical Library Association, and FIOCRUZ in Rio De Janeiro. Lee has been invited to serve as an international advisor to the Board of Medicine and Health Internet Applications Group in Brazil. He also owns three discussion groups: HMATRIX-L, a discussion of on-line resources; CPRI-L, a discussion of computerized medical records; and MMA-TRIX-L, the official American Medical Informatics Association Internet Working Group discussion list.

Lee Hancock
Bitnet: le07144@ukanvm
Internet: lhancock@kumc.wpo.ukans.edu

Physicians' Guide to the Internet

Lee Hancock

University of Kansas Medical Center
Educational Technology
Archie R. Dykes Library
Kansas City, Kansas

Lippincott - Raven
PUBLISHERS
Philadelphia • New York

Lippincott - Raven Publishers, 227 East Washington Square, Philadelphia, Pennsylvania 19106-3780

Made in the United States of America

Library of Congress Cataloging-in-Publication Data

Hancock, Lee.
    Physicians' Guide to the Internet / Lee Hancock
       p.   cm.
    Includes bibliographical references and index.
    ISBN 0-397-51634-7
    1. Medicine—Computer network resources. 2. Internet (Computer network) 3. Internet
(Computer network) I. Title.
    [DNLM: 1. Computer Communications Networks. 2. Medical Informatics. W26.5 H234p 1995]
    R118.H25 1995
    025.06′61—dc20
    DNLM/DLC
    for Library of Congress
                                            95-32101
                                             CIP

The material contained in this volume was submitted as previously unpublished material, except in the instances in which credit has been given to the source from which some of the illustrative material was derived.

Great care has been taken to maintain the accuracy of the information contained in the volume. However, neither Lippincott - Raven Publishers nor the authors can be held responsible for errors or for any consequences arising from the use of the information contained herein.

9 8 7 6 5 4 3 2 1

The publisher cannot guarantee the suitability or accuracy of information, or the availability of resources listed in this book. All information contained herein is subject to change. Mention of a specific product or company does not imply an endorsement.

To those physicians finding the courage to make that first step into the Internet, to those whose curiosity has been rewarded with the wonders of cyberspace, and to those experienced explorers already suffering from information overload.

Contents

PART ONE: THE BASICS

PART TWO: THE GUIDE

Foreword

AN INTRODUCTION TO THE MEDICAL INTERNET

Medical Internet Growth Trends

Physicians and other healthcare professionals are rapidly joining the more than 20 million users and 20,000 networks that make up the Internet. This high level of connectivity presents unprecedented opportunities for global cooperation, networking, information access, and sharing in improving patient care. The recent introduction of graphical Mosaic-type interfaces from Netscape and the national on-line services make the Internet attractive and accessible to this new audience. Large numbers of medical practitioners are beginning to share medical knowledge on many disease and therapy topics. Medical institutions, universities, and medically oriented commercial enterprises are rushing to establish "Web pages" on the Internet. The Internet draws on these individuals and resource providers to offer a rich support network and an immense database of digital information for those interested in the fields of health and medicine.

Practical Uses

Currently, medical practitioners can search world-wide databases of text, dermatologic and pathologic slides, radiographic images, and multimedia learning modules and display these to personal computer screens within seconds. Special interest groups are rapidly creating directories, newsgroups, and mailing lists of medical knowledge. News, product information, and conference announcements are being made available on the Internet well before they can arrive by print media. Internet communication is particularly rich regarding computers and medicine, academic research, and information technologies. A parallel development of Internet clinical medicine uses is taking place as practitioners join the Internet and exchange new developments, case studies, treatment protocols, employment opportunities, and remote consultations.

Potential Uses

Medical research, diagnosis, and therapy require urgent access and integration of information from vast databases. Medical applications of the Internet and healthworker networking are a huge, underdeveloped global resource. One can envision that through data transfers and videoconferencing the breadth of human knowledge, the wisdom of distributed experts, and the analytic ability of high-speed computing can be applied to any clinical practice issue. The Internet "Web browsers" and interactive forums bring this vision within reach.

The Hancock List

Since 1990, Lee Hancock has been part of the pioneering efforts to encourage medical applications of the Internet and to index Internet medical resources through his "Hancock List" of health science resources. This compendium updates Lee's voluntary efforts to produce and distribute the list. The number of medical resources offered in this current version has expanded dramatically from previous versions. Internet explorers will find it valuable to have these resources available as a companion text to on-line exploration. The resources can be accessed by entering their "Uniform Resource Locators" (URLs) on any Internet Web browser. It is hoped that text will encourage the entry of medical practitioners onto the Internet. A key feature of the Internet is the potential for every user to become a resource or information provider. Participation and knowledge sharing has the potential to focus an unlimited wealth of text and multimedia information to improve patient care.

Gary Malet
gmalet@surfer.win.net
Family Physician
Healthtel Corporation
Stockton, California; and
Chair
American Medical Informatics Association
Internet Working Group

Preface

The purpose of the *Physicians' Guide to the Internet* is to provide a list of Internet resources dealing with health, disease, therapy, and clinical medicine. As the title suggests, the primary audience is the physician, whether in private practice or with an educational institution. The *Guide* is designed for members of the medical community who may be new to on-line communication, as well as for the experienced Internet explorer. It offers a brief introduction to the Internet, a guide to Internet connectivity, a description of the navigation tools required to find your way around the vast resources on the "Net," and a list of medical resources to get you started.

This book does not attempt to be exhaustive. Information not directly related to clinical practice, such as patient support groups, medical student concerns, or biological research sources, are not covered. Those resources certainly exist in abundance on the Net and can be found in the Internet Health Science Resources List mentioned later.

This *Guide* includes the basic information needed to access the medical resources listed; it is not intended to be a one-stop, how-to-explore-the-Internet reference. For those who want to learn more about the Internet, there are a plethora of books that can teach you to navigate, search, and put your own information online. (See *Bibliography* for author's favorite references.)

This book is an attempt to break down the barriers that face the health community in taking advantage of the Internet information explosion. While every effort has been made to verify the resources listed here, there is no guarantee that everything will still be available by the time this *Guide* is in print. Likewise, there is and will continue to be much that is not found here. The Internet is a volatile, growing entity. This is especially true of discussion groups and World Wide Web "home pages" discussed later, with new information sites appearing daily.

It is this author's hope that what you find in the pages of this book will whet your appetite for exploring a new communication-/information-collecting tool. The Internet is bringing information into our homes and offices, right to the desktop. Enjoy.

Acknowledgments

A project of this type involves so many people that it's difficult to know where to start saying thanks. Certainly I owe thanks to Dr. Gary Malet for writing the foreword to this book and for his continuing support throughout this project. My gratitude also goes out to Jenny Jacobson (jenny@cadre.dsl.pitt.edu) for designing a database using Microsoft Access to simplify the tracking and categorizing of Internet medical resources. Both Dr. Malet and Ms. Jacobson continually pass on new-found Internet resources for my database. For their efforts and friendship, I thank them. Then there is the 1,200-person membership of HMATRIX-L discussion group (List-serv@www.kumc.edu), through whose eyes and ears I learn and whose leads I follow. To all of you, thank you for sharing.

Glossary of Common Internet Terms

Archie
An electronic index of files found on anonymous file transfer protocol (FTP) sites. Keyword-searchable in both file name and description.

backbone
A high-capacity links that serve as the primary framework for the Internet globally.

BITNET (Because It's Time Network)
The grandfather of the Internet. BITNET is a mail only network and is the primary source of discussion groups known as *Listserv Lists*.

BBS
Bulletin Board System

DNS (Domain Name System)
An electronic mail addressing system used in networks such as the Internet and BITNET. The Internet DNS consists of a hierarchical sequence of names, from the most specific to the most general (left to right), separated by dots. Example: NIC.DDN.MIL.

FAQ
Frequently Asked Question

FTP (File Transfer Protocol)
The File Transfer Protocol is a method of sending files to and receiving files from a remote computer on the Internet. It is also the name of a program that uses the protocol to transfer files.

Gopher
A world-wide information service with many implementations, Gopher works as a top-level, subject-oriented menu system that accesses other information

services across the Internet. It retrieves information from Internet connections and arranges it in a hierarchy with each item representing either a file or a directory. The telneting or FTPs are transparent to the user.

GUI

Graphical user interface

HTML (Hypertext Markup Language)

Used to produce a hypertext document for display by a World Wide Web browser. HTML uses a standardized set of tags that tells the browser how to display the text as well as to specify hypertext links.

HTTP (Hypertext Transfer Protocol)

A protocol that defines hypertext links to information on the World Wide Web.

LAN

Local area network

Listserv

An automated mailing list distribution system enabling on-line discussions conducted by electronic mail throughout the Internet. The Listserv program was originally designed for the BITNET/EARN (European Academic and Research Network) networks.

Lynx

A text-only World Wide Web browser for any vt100 emulating terminal program using full screen, arrow keys, highlighting, etc. Fast navigation of cross-linked hypertext documents (not multimedia) over a low-speed dial-up connection. Originated at the University of Kansas.

NCSA Mosaic

Developed at the National Center for Supercomputing Applications (NCSA), Mosaic is a World Wide Web browser that allows easy point-and-click graphical hypermedia access to the World Wide Web over a SLIP (Serial Line Internet Protocol) or PPP (Point-to-Point Protocol) connection. Mosaic runs on X Windows, Macintosh, and Microsoft Windows, and has integrated transparent access to all other Inernet services.

PPP/SLIP

Point-to-Point Protocol/Serial Line Internet Protocol

TCP/IP (Transmission Control Protocol/Internet Protocol)

The basic protocol that allows information to be distributed over the Internet.

Telnet

A protocol on the Internet that allows remote logins to another computer system. It is also a program that allows a user to browse menus, read text files, use Gopher services, and search on-line databases using the Telnet protocol.

URL (Uniform Resource Locator)

A standard for specifying the address of a document on the Internet, such as a home page, a file or a newsgroup.

Usenet

A global bulletin board of sorts, in which millions of people exchange public information on a great variety of topics.

Veronica

A service on the Internet that maintains an index of Gopher items and provides keyword searches of those titles. The result of a search is a set of Gopher-type data items, which is returned to the user as a Gopher menu.

WAIS (Wide-Area Information Servers)

A powerful search and retrieval system for gathering information across the Internet.

WWW (World Wide Web)

The World Wide Web is a hypertext-based system that provides top level access to various documents, lists, and services on the Internet. With a Graphical User Interface such as Mosaic, the WWW allows the creation and transfer of multimedia objects. It requires interactive access to the Internet.

Physicians' Guide to the Internet

1

The Medical Internet

Imagine the following scenario: A rural oncologist wants to find out what investigational cancer chemotherapy protocols are available for his worried young patient with metastatic breast cancer. From his desktop computer, he dials an 800 number and "logs onto" an Internet provider. From among his many electronic "bookmarks" he selects CANCERNET, a free, government-funded service reporting chemotherapy protocols, investigational new drugs, and availability of those drugs. The oncologist knows this information is the most current available because the service is electronic, updated monthly, and peer-reviewed. Fantasy? No, CANCERNET exists today. You (and your patients) can have access to current information right now.

Millions of individuals communicate daily over the Internet, exchanging ideas by words, pictures, and sound. The Internet is the closest functioning network to the envisioned "global electronic highway." It may eventually evolve to become the foundation of a universal data highway available to all homes. One can easily envision a future in which rural physicians can send x-rays, heart sounds, and video clips of patients to specialists in major hospitals for diagnosis or discussion. Continuing education courses may be offered from major medical schools via the Internet. The global electronic highway is almost complete.

No print medium can keep up with the rapid expansion of the Internet. It can provide only a starting place, a reference point from which to expand knowledge of on-line resources. For the most part, Internet resources are available through voluntary efforts. They may come online only to disappear at the whim of the person who owns the information. Careers take new directions, interests change, resources find new homes or go offline. By far the best place to learn about Internet medical resources is "the Net" itself. An excellent place to start is the discussion group:

HMATRIX-L@WWW.KUMC.EDU

This is a discussion group concerning Internet and other online resources. Another source of new information is

NEW-LIST@VM1.NODAK.EDU

Almost all new discussion groups are announced on this list. Of course, the announcements include all subjects, not just those concerned with medicine.

The entries in this Guide have been selected from the author's Internet Health Science Resources List. This comprehensive electronic document has been available since 1989 on various file transfer protocol (FTP) sites. It is updated a couple of times a year as a strictly volunteer project. The most recent version can be found at

FTP2.CC.UKANS.EDU

in the directory *pub/hmatrix* and as the file *medlst04.zip*. (The *04* indicates the month of the release and will change with updates.) To access the document, login as **anonymous** and use your electronic mail (e-mail) address as the password.

The following two chapters provide basic information on how to access the Internet and the tools required to find your way around. Chapter 4 contains a selection of Internet health and medical resources organized by subject.

The following conventions are used in this book:

Bold type is used to indicate commands that are typed or executed by the user and to highlight the names of Internet resources.

Italic type is used to indicate file names and directories.

E-mail addresses are in UPPER CASE TYPE for ease of reading, but are not case sensitive.

Uniform resource locators (URLs) are case-sensitive and should be typed as written.

2

Accessing the Internet

When Vice President Gore dubbed the Internet the *Information Super Highway*, he coined the buzzword of the 1990s. Most people still call it *the Internet*. Though it is getting easier, finding the type of Internet connection that is right for you requires some thought. Why pay for services you will not use? The first consideration should be your personal or professional communication requirements. Do you want to transfer files between computer systems throughout the world? Do you need to browse other computer systems such as those maintained by university libraries? Are you interested in exploring the new multimedia technologies just beginning to flood the World Wide Web (WWW)? Or are you interested just in sending e-mail to friends and colleagues? This type of needs assessment will determine what kind of services you will need to look for in an Internet provider.

Connecting to the Internet requires a number of components, with several options, depending on the depth of service you need. Fortunately, as the popularity of the Internet increases, those options for access can only increase. What the user needs is all components delivered in one package, not multiple options for each. I will mention some of those packages a little later. Let us first start at the beginning—hardware and software for Internet connectivity.

HARDWARE

Any personal computer can connect to the Internet, but the type of Internet services you want will depend, to some extent, on how much computing power you have. Any old IBM-compatible personal computer (PC) or Macintosh SE will work just fine for e-mail or file transfer, but to really "surf" the Net, a much higher-end computer is required. This is because the graphical user interfaces (GUIs) being developed, such as Mosaic and Netscape (the most popular World Wide Web browsers), require at least 4 megabytes of random access memory (RAM) to run at usable speeds on either Windows or Macintosh computers.

3

No matter what kind of desktop computer you use, there are two methods of connecting to the Internet: through a local area network (LAN) or by dial-in access through a telephone modem. Most institutions connected to the Internet use the former. Individual desktop computers, which are given unique Internet protocol (IP) addresses, are attached to a local server via the LAN. That local server provides the connection to the Internet backbone. Of course, the actual technical configuration varies from institution to institution.

Connecting to the Internet via a home or office stand-alone computer requires a modem. A modem is used to transmit digital information from a computer through ordinary phone lines to a network provider or Internet access provider. All modems work basically the same way and are generally packaged with the communication software needed to make them work. An internal modem fits into a slot inside the computer, whereas an external modem sits outside the computer with its own power supply and connects to the serial port on a PC or to the modem port on a Macintosh. The type you select is a personal choice or is dictated by your computer's configuration. I suggest consulting with a local computer "guru" before making a purchase.

While there are many aspects to selecting a modem, perhaps the most important in terms of Internet access is speed. Modem speed is measured in bits per second (BPS). Without getting technical, a bit is the smallest amount of information a computer will recognize. The more bits your modem can send and receive, the faster the information will travel over the phone lines. Currently, you can get a 14,400-bps modem for about $150, which is the minimum speed needed to take advantage of the GUI interface. Most come packaged with communication software such as Bitcom or Procomm. If you have an "e-mail only" service, a slower 2,400-bps modem will suffice but is not recommended. If you choose to buy a separate communication software package, be sure it will support vt100 terminal emulation and Kermit or Zmodem file transfers. This ensures that your software can "talk" to the mainframe computer with which you will eventually be communicating.

SOFTWARE

If you choose a provider that offers full access to the Internet, you will also need the following software in order to take advantage of the GUI interface:

- World Wide Web browser—a Hypertext Markup Language (HTML) browser that allows users to access World Wide Web home pages. Netscape and Mosaic are the most widely known as of this writing.

- TCP/IP Stack—TCP/IP is the Internet's communication protocol. The TCP/IP stack is the software that, when loaded on a PC, interprets the information that is sent to and from the Internet.
- SLIP/PPP or LAN drivers—SLIP and PPP are two protocols that allow dial-up access to the Internet through a serial link over normal phone lines. The LAN driver is used to connect directly to your local area network.

Although gathering all this software and configuring it on your computer used to be an arduous and often frustrating task, several "all-in-one" Internet packages are now on the market. Packages like Internet in a Box, developed by SPRY, Inc. for the Windows environment, contain all the necessary software you need to access the Internet from your home or office. This prepackaged Internet access software was developed for novice installation. With independent software packages, you still have to choose an Internet access provider. Many providers are also giving subscribers their own version of desktop computer software. For example, NETCOM, a major Internet provider, has developed NetCruiser for Windows (Macintosh version to be released soon), a full set of Internet tools available for use on its system (see Appendix A for a listing of Internet access software packages).

ACCESS

The most common means of Internet access is through an institution of higher education. If you or your hospital is affiliated with a university, chances are you already have an Internet connection. Many private hospitals are also beginning to see the advantage of bringing Internet access to their employees. If you are not sure, check with your computer center for local information.

Finding a commercial Internet service provider is getting easier and less expensive every day, due to increasing competition for your on-line dollar. These are called *dial-in accounts* because users dial-in to the host using a computer and modem. As with any competitive business, there is a wide variety of services, and the associated costs vary greatly. We will begin with the most popular use of the Internet, e-mail.

Virtually all Internet providers offer e-mail. Obviously, if this is all that interests you, your connectivity options broaden considerably. So we will look at those options first.

Begin by checking out your local bulletin board system (BBS). The number of BBSs offering e-mail to the Internet is growing steadily. Because these are small enterprises, accounts can range in price from a few dollars to $50 or so per month. Finding the right local BBS may take some detective work.

Check your local computer store for a list. Most cities also have a local computer publication which lists BBSs.

Another option is to sign up with one of the major commercial on-line services. America Online (800-827-6364), CompuServe (800-858-0411), Genie (800-638-9636), and Prodigy (800-776-3449) all offer e-mail to and from the Internet. Of course, these services charge a monthly fee and some connect time charges, which vary with the provider and the subscription package. America Online and Prodigy also offer access to Usenet "newsgroups" (discussed later). All these services are expanding to include full Internet services.

Another option is Delphi (800-695-4005), a nationwide Internet provider and on-line service. Delphi offers full access to Internet tools using a menu-based interface. There is usually a local phone number in most major U.S. cities.

Another choice, especially for rural areas, is access through a packet switching network such as MCI Mail or SprintNet. They provide each customer with an Internet address and an 800 telephone number to use. These networks usually carry an hourly charge or a yearly fee (about $30) plus a charge per message. With some, there is no charge to receive mail, so shop around.

Of course, there is much more to the Internet than e-mail. There are 5,000-plus Usenet newsgroups to follow, Gopher servers to burrow through, FTP sites bulging with software, graphics and information, and a whole World Wide Web to explore (see Chapter 3 for an explanation of these tools). If you want full Internet access, there are a couple of options, depending on where you live. Unfortunately, there is still relatively little connectivity beyond e-mail in rural areas.

Freenets are a recent development and are gaining in popularity everywhere. These are like community-based bulletin board systems with e-mail, information services, and usually at least some Internet services. Freenets are operated under a concept much like public television, in that they are privately and community-supported. They offer dial-in access and are, as the name indicates, free. How much Internet access they provide depends on the freenet.

A second option is to find a public access provider in your area or one that uses an 800 number for dial-in. Besides checking with your local computer store, there a couple of easy ways to do this. Check the local BBSs for a file called *PDIAL* (public dialup Internet access list). This is a list of Internet access and service providers by area code. If you have e-mail through one of the services described above, you can get the latest copy by sending e-mail to:

INFO-DELI-SERVER@PDIAL.COM

with the subject line containing the phrase **Send PDIAL.**

A second option is to contact the Internet Network Information Center (InterNIC) and ask about Internet access providers in your area:

InterNic Information Services
General Atomics
P.O. Box #85608
San Diego, CA 92186-9784
Phone: (800) 444-4345
E-mail: info@is.internic.com

Service provider rates vary greatly depending on the time of access, speed of access desired, and several other factors. Again, it pays to shop around (see Appendix B for a list of Internet access providers listed by state).

3

Internet Navigation Tools

The Internet is a network of networks all working together to form a global community. The Internet uses unique addresses and tools (i.e., computer software) to let you virtually visit faraway places and move information around the world. This chapter is an introduction to Internet navigation tools.

The Internet provides three basic tools of exploration:

- E-mail The primary means of Internet communication
- Remote login (Telnet) For browsing another computer
- File Transfer Protocol (Best known as FTP. You will seldom see it spelled out.) For transferring files between computers

Within that context there are at least six popular vehicles used to post, view, and retrieve information and files on the Internet. Each is briefly discussed in this chapter. For those wanting a more detailed explanation of how the Internet works, a bibliography of this explorer's favorite books is provided.

INTERNET ADDRESSES

Just like in the real world, the virtual world requires an address to navigate. We will look briefly at how Internet addresses work.

Today's Internet uses three addressing schemes:

- Domain Name System (DNS)
- E-mail
- Universal Resource Locator (URL)

This is not as confusing as it sounds. Each has a specific purpose. Let us begin with the DNS, which is the foundation of all Internet addresses.

Every computer node attached to the Internet has a unique numerical address known as Internet Protocol (IP) address. To the computer it would look something like this: 129.237.28.3. Unfortunately, most humans have trouble remembering numerical sequences. This is where the DNS comes to the rescue. A name server translates an IP address into a text or name address like this:

UKANVM.CC.UKANS.EDU

This represents a node, which is a specific computer. Like your street address, each part has a specific meaning. From left to right the address goes from specific to general, just like your street address goes from top to bottom, specific to general. A DNS address breaks down like this:

UKANVM The name of the local computer

CC   A subdomain. In this case it means *computer center*

UKANS   Another subdomain, here referring to *University of Kansas*.

EDU   The domain or type of institution (others are *GOV* for government, *MIL* for military, *COM* for commercial, etc.).

All Internet addressing, regardless of the interface used (to be discussed later), is based on the DNS.

An e-mail address has two parts, a user identification (user-ID) and a node, joined together by the "@" sign. This sounds simple enough, but it can be quite complicated. Sometimes the address can look as simple as:

LHANCOCK@UKANAIX.CC.UKANS.EDU

where the user-ID is *LHANCOCK* and the node *UKANAIX.CC.UKANS.EDU* (which is one of the nodes for the University of Kansas). Sometimes an address can be filled with odd symbols like "!%" or similar characters designed to guide the message between various smaller local area networks.

The Universal Resource Locator is the "new kid" in cyberspace. Developed in Switzerland to navigate a new service, the World Wide Web (WWW), the URL is rapidly becoming the standardized addressing scheme. Bear in mind that URLs require the use of a Web browser. A typical URL looks like this:

http://www.mit.edu:8001/people/samajane/home.html

This happens to be the address of a WWW site for brain tumor survivors called Samantha's HEADquarters. (Unlike e-mail addresses, URLs are case-sensitive, so *Samajane* is not the same as *samajane*.)

As with other Internet addresses, there is a method to what appears at first glance to be madness. It breaks down like this:

access_type://domain.name/directory_name/file.name

Using the Samantha's HEADquarters URL mentioned above, the address is broken down as follows:

http:// This represents World Wide Web access

www.mit.edu:8001 In this case, the physical location is MIT (*:8001* represents the connection port; this part of the URL is used only when required by a particular system.)

people/samajane/home.html This is the directory path to a file called *home.html*. (HTML files are discussed in the World Wide Web section.)

Other access_types are:

gopher:// To access Gopher sites

ftp:// To access FTP sites

news: To access Usenet news. (Notice the absence of "//" for this access_type.)

ELECTRONIC MAIL

Exchanging e-mail with colleagues is probably the best way to become comfortable with the electronic world. Sending electronic mail across international networks is almost as easy as sending paper mail. And it usually takes only minutes to arrive. The Internet also makes use of e-mail in a system called *Listserv discussion groups*.

Listserv Lists

The Internet has thousands of special interest groups called *lists*. These Listserv (shortened from list server) programs exist on the mainframe computers of universities and corporations throughout the world. There are about

300 medically oriented discussion lists concerning various specialties and diseases, and the list is growing rapidly. Any individual with e-mail to the outside world may "subscribe" to a list electronically, and any mail posted to the list is distributed to all subscribers. Imagine asking 300 of your colleagues around the world a question concerning a diagnosis and receiving an answer within minutes, or discussing U.S. health care reform with health workers from other nations.

Listserv is simply e-mail distribution software (Fig. 1). The original Listserv software was written by Eric Thomas for the IBM mainframe VM/CMS operating system, although the term *Listserv* has evolved into a generic name for all e-mail distribution software that has been developed for various mainframe operating systems. It currently seems that only Internet purists distinguish between Listserv and the Unix Listproc and Majordomo software, or the U.K.'s Mailbase program. Is this distinction important? Of course, there is the ethical consideration of crediting software titles and authors, but there is a second consideration for the user—although all server software appears to be similar, there are important differences. For example, the **subscribe** command is the same for Listserv and Listproc, but to get a list of subscribers the command is **review** for Listserv and **recipient** for Listproc. A summary of

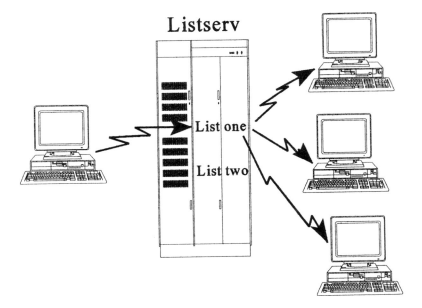

FIG. 1. Listserv

the different mail server commands can be found in Appendix C.

Generally, Listserv discussion groups can be divided into two types: layperson-oriented and professionally oriented. An example of the former is the list:

DIET (DIET@INDYCMS)

a wellness, exercise, and diet discussion forum.

While these are health-oriented discussion lists, they attract people from all backgrounds, including many students. Professionally oriented lists include such forums as:

WYTSENDO (WYTSENDO@DARTCMS1) A discussion of all aspects of the disease endometriosis

MEDLIB-L (MEDLIB-L@UBVM) A discussion group for medical librarians

EMFLDS-L (EMFLDS-L@UBVM) A forum for electromagnetic uses in medicine, science, and communications

To join one of these mailing lists, one must "subscribe" to the list by sending the server an e-mail message. Of course, you can "unsubscribe" from a list you no longer find interesting. E-mail is not case-sensitive: HEALTHRE is the same as healthre.

In most cases, one can send a message to a server, which will automatically add your name to the distribution list. For example, to subscribe to HEALTHRE@UKCC.UKY.EDU, a discussion group concerning health care reform, send an e-mail message to:

LISTSERV@UKCC.UKY.EDU

leave the *from* and *subject* lines blank. You are sending mail to a computer, not a person.

In the first line of the message, type:

subscribe HEALTHRE your name

Likewise, when you wish to shut off the mail coming from this group, send the message:

unsubscribe HEALTHRE

to the same address. Note that your name is not needed to unsubscribe.

Once you are a member of this mailing list, messages can be sent to all the subscribers by addressing the message to the group, i.e., sending the message to:

HEALTHRE@UKCC.UKY.EDU

Be forewarned, some active lists may generate twenty or more messages a day. If you are paying for a connection that charges for messages received, it could get expensive. Also, as in any community, the virtual community has certain rules and etiquette. Before jumping into any discussion, read (or in Net parlance, "lurk") for a while to get the gist of things. It may save some embarrassment.

Usenet Newsgroups

"Newsgroups" are topical discussion special interest groups, similar in many ways to Listserv discussion groups. Unlike Listserv lists, where one has to subscribe to receive messages by e-mail, the "posts" in the Usenet groups are stored on the mainframe computer for a period of time. Some Listserv discussions are also "echoed" to the news groups. Just about every topic imaginable is covered somewhere in a Usenet newsgroup. While not technically part of the Internet, Usenet Newsgroups are generally available through Unix computers connected to the Internet (Fig. 2). They are like an uncensored orphan of the Internet and a great source of information and fun. There are more than 5,000 topics covered, with new ones being added and outdated ones deleted daily. How long they stay in the system depends on the system operator; most purge old messages every few weeks.

A newsreader program is used to access the messages for reading. There are many news readers, each with a different look, that are provided by Internet access providers or come bundled in Internet software packages. Like Listserv lists, Usenet newsgroups are usually free to the person connected to the Internet.

Among the many medical newsgroups can be found:

sci.med A discussion of almost any medically related subject

sci.med.radiology A discussion of radiology issues

sci.med.telemedicine A discussion of telemedicine practices and issues

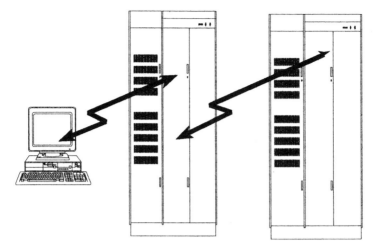

FIG. 2. Usenet News Groups

As users post messages locally to these newsgroups, the messages are re-layed throughout the Net to institutions that subscribe to that newsgroup.

A close cousin of Usenet newsgroups is the electronic publication. While they do not invite discussion, most are subscribed to and distributed in the same manner as the discussion groups. Many electronic publications are distributed free to subscribers across the Internet. They vary in frequency, but all offer timely information to the medical community and most welcome reader interaction. A few examples include:

HEALTH INFOCOM NEWSLETTER (LISTSERV@ASUACAD) A weekly newsletter of medical information

To subscribe, send e-mail with the first line of message being:
subscribe MEDNEWS your name

HANDICAP DIGEST (LISTSERV@NDSUVM1) Articles relating to all is-sues affecting the handicapped (irregular frequency)

To subscribe, send e-mail to WTM@BUNKER.SHEL.ISC-BR.COM and request to be added to the mail distribution.

SBIS NEWSLETTER (EMP@BRFASPESP.BITNET) A bimonthly news pub-lication of the Brazilian Society for Health Informatics

Send e-mail to EMP@BRFAPESP.BITNET and request to be added to the mailing list.

REMOTE LOGIN

Remote login means operating a computer, usually a mainframe, at a remote site from your home or office. It could be anywhere in the world. The Internet provides two basic types of remote login; Telnet and FTP. With the development of GUIs, typing complex commands and having to know enough Unix to navigate the system is becoming a thing of the past, but Telnet and FTP are going on behind the scenes.

Telnet

Telnet is simply remote login and can be thought of like going to the library without a card—only browsing is available, and no files can be transferred (Fig. 3). Telnet allows the user to connect to a remote computer to search databases, read text, explore library catalogs, and much more. Login procedures are specific to each site. No uniform procedures have been established, but on-

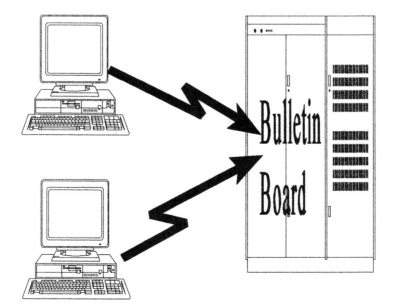

FIG. 3. Telnet

line help is usually available by typing **help** or **?**, and most use some type of menu system to help the user navigate through the data. For example, the BIOETHICS ONLINE SERVICE (min.lib.mcw.edu) is a Telnet site provided by the Center for the Study of Bioethics and The Health Information Technology Center of the Medical College of Wisconsin. It contains current information concerning ethics and law pertaining to the health and medical fields. Another particularly interesting Telnet site is FEDWORLD (telnet://fedworld.gov). This is an entry point into almost all federal government-maintained databases, including a dozen or so òf interest to the medical profession.

File Transfer Protocol

File transfer protocol is analogous to entering a library with a card. The user is free to browse through a remote computer and take any public file of interest. File transfer protocol is used to transfer both text and binary (nontext) files over the Internet from one computer to another anywhere in the world (Fig. 4).

There are two kinds of FTP sessions, personal and anonymous. To transfer a file to a colleague—a personal transfer—either the sender or receiver must

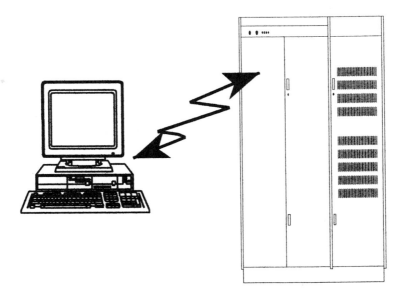

FIG. 4. File Transfer Protocol (FTP)

be authorized to logon to the other's account. Access to a personal account requires a password.

Anonymous FTP, which is open to the public, is so named because the login is the word **anonymous** (lower case). The primary use of FTP is anonymous. Certain computer sites act as repositories of information by storing vast numbers of files. There are more than 700 anonymous FTP sites open to anyone who has Internet access. These sites hold freeware and shareware productivity and educational software, as well as informational text files, graphics, sound files, and movie clips.

For example, nuclear medicine-related files are stored on a file server at the University of Western Ontario. If your computer has FTP software, you can FTP to UWOVAX.UWO.CA. Nuclear medicine files are stored in a directory called: *PUB:[00000.NUCMED]*.

File transfer works like this:

1. A user logs onto a local mainframe computer connected to the Internet.
2. Using FTP, a direct link is established to a remote mainframe computer, known as an *anonymous FTP site.*
3. Login as **anonymous**; the requested password is usually the user-id [user identification (e-mail address)]. Most FTP sites are Unix-based, so all commands, including **anonymous**, are case-sensitive.
4. The user can look at directories on the remote computer using the commands **dir** (directory) and **cd** (change directories) to select files to transfer to the local mainframe.
5. Once a file is selected, the command **get** *filename* will transfer the file to the local computer, for example: **get** *readme.txt.*
6. To logoff type **quit**.

These basic commands will work on Unix-based FTP sites. Be aware that most, but not all, FTP sites are Unix. The process remains the same, but the screen will look different. Also the FTP software or interface you use to connect to the site will affect the look of the screen and the steps needed to transfer the file. Some nice interfaces have been developed for the Macintosh (Fetch) and Windows (Ws-FTP) that provide a simple point-and-click file transfer. These programs require either a direct Internet connection or a SLIP/PPP type of connection.

GOPHER

Internet Gophers are information servers that present you with a hierarchical menu of resources in a simple, consistent manner. The advantage of using a Gopher server is that the software handles all the DNS addresses as well as Telnet and FTP commands. Internet navigation becomes a matter of reading menus (Fig. 5).

Developed by the Computer and Information Services group at the University of Minnesota (the gopher is the school mascot) during the mid 1980s, Gopher was the first serious attempt to bring a simple, practical user interface to the Internet. The software was made available free to educational institutions throughout the world. Because of their ease of use, Gopher servers spread throughout the Internet during the late 1980s and early 1990s.

Gopher is a client/server system. A Gopher "client" can reside on your personal computer or on a mainframe at your site, depending on how you access the Net. Gopher clients are also included in most Internet software packages. By choosing menu options, the client connects to a remote Gopher server, which then presents the user with a series of menus for further exploration. Gopher also supports FTP for downloading files. Gopher's "bookmark" feature allows the user to save site addresses in a file with the click of a mouse.

University- and government-supported Gophers contain a wealth of medical- and health-related information, and publishers are starting to put their catalogs on Gopher servers. A list of medical school Gophers is provided in Chapter 4.

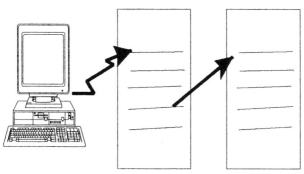

Top Level Menu Sub Menu

FIG. 5. Gopher

WORLD WIDE WEB (WWW)

One of the more exciting new concepts for exploring the Internet is the World Wide Web, which is overtaking Gopher in popularity at lightning speed. The difference between Gopher and WWW is that the Web supports hypertext and multimedia capabilities. Hypertext documents are information sources that contain links to other related documents. The World Wide Web has been described as a "wide-area hypermedia information retrieval initiative" aiming to give universal access to a large universe of documents (Fig. 6).

"The Web" was created at the European Centre of Particle Physics (CERN) in Switzerland. While there are similarities between Gopher and the Web, their differences are phenomenal. Both tools allow the user to browse information across the Internet without requiring login or cryptic commands, but the Web is much more flexible. While Gopher is a structured system of menus, the Web looks like a text document. This means that *home pages*, as Web sites are called, can hold the text formatting, making them easier to read and more attractive. Furthermore, World Wide Web documents are written in HTML, which provides the ability to create hypertext links to other documents. Selecting highlighted areas within a WWW document using a mouse or keystroke opens another document located somewhere else on the Internet. Al-

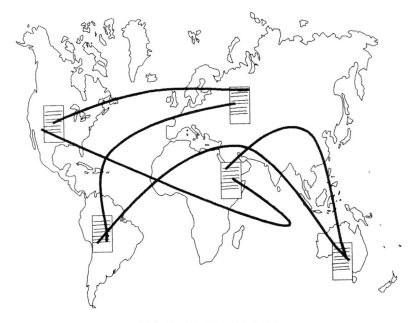

FIG. 6. World Wide Web

though the document could be on a computer in a remote part of the world, its physical location is irrelevant to the user.

With the proper helper applications, multimedia capabilities add a new dimension to Internet exploration. Graphics, sounds, and movie clips can be previewed online before downloading to your computer. A hypertext document can also link in graphics, movies, and sound, giving almost unlimited versatility. The Web is also compatible with all other Internet tools, e.g., Gopher servers, FTP, Telnet, and Usenet. Perhaps more importantly, because of the standardization developed for the HTML documents, anyone with access to a Web server can easily create a personal home page. For the first time in history, individuals can make information instantly accessible to any user world-wide.

ONCOLINK (http://cancer.med.upenn.edu) is an excellent example of this. Because his daughter has leukemia, Loren Buhel, Jr., PhD, developed ONCOLINK to provide current cancer information to physicians, social workers, patients, and their supporters. This site was developed and maintained in Dr. Buhel's spare time and is a proven success of what one person can do with a little knowledge of HTML. ONCOLINK has developed into a major resource for oncology information on the Internet.

As discussed in Chapter 2, the GUIs or "browser" clients that are needed to access the Web need a lot of computing power. The two most popular Web browsers as of this writing are the National Center for Super Computing Applications' (NCSA) Mosaic and Netscape Communications Corporation's Netscape Navigator. Both are available as freeware over the Internet and both have a Windows and Macintosh version. To use these and other browsers satisfactorily, the user must have either a direct connection to the Internet backbone or a SLIP/PPP type of a connection, a high-speed modem, and a relatively high-end computer (minimum of 4 MB of RAM). Another option is to Telnet to a public server, which provides only the text of the document (because no GUI is used) and no multimedia components. Two such servers are:

CERN info.cern.ch (no username needed)

The University of Kansas ukanaix.cc.ukans.edu (login as **www**)

The Internet is constantly a work in progress, with new features being added daily and old resources being updated. There are new searchable indices for Listservs, Gophers, and World Wide Web sites so that the new user can track down sources of information rather than depending on stumbling across them.

To make these data warehouses more "user-accessible," better front-end programs must be developed. World Wide Web browsers such as Netscape are a step in this direction.

4

Internet Medical Resources

The latest statistic I have run across says the Internet is doubling in size and traffic every two months. While medical resources are not expanding at that pace, new announcements are a daily occurrence. Because of the time constraints and deadlines of publishing much of what is "out there" is not included here. This is especially true of World Wide Web home pages and Listserv discussion groups. Both of these resources are coming online at a staggering rate as the medical community discovers the Net. The following are resources available to you, mostly free of charge. I hope you find the Internet as fascinating and as useful as I have.

All resource addresses, with the exception of e-mail, are listed as URLs.

DISEASES/DISORDERS

AIDS

AIDS
Access: E-mail
AIDS@CS.UCLA.EDU

This is a redistribution list for the Usenet newsgroup Sci.Med.AIDS. Mail to the list is automatically forwarded to the moderator team for the newsgroup.

Owner: Moderator Team
RUTVM1@RUTGERS.EDU

AIDS ALERT FOR HEALTH CARE WORKERS

Access: Send e-mail to the owner requesting to be added to the distribution list
Owner: Bob Jackson
LIBR8508@RYERSON

AIDS Alert for Health Care Workers is an index to journal articles and occasional papers that address the occupational health and safety concerns of health care workers who are providing care for patients with AIDS. The *Alert* is annotated and compiled by Charlotte Broome of the Ryerson Polytechnical Institute's Education and Life Sciences Library. Issues of the *Alert* will appear three to four times per year. The *Alert* is distributed electronically by the Institute for AIDS Information.
Correspondence: Ryerson Polytechnical Institute
Library, Education & Life Sciences
350 Victoria Street, Toronto,
Ontario, Canada M5B 2K3

AIDS ONLINE DATABASES

Access: Word Wide Web
http://www.nlm.nih.gov/top_level.dir/nlm_online_info.html

The 75,000 members of the NLM international on-line database network may now search AIDSLINE, AIDSDRUGS, AIDSTRIALS, and DIRLINE without charge. In the past, fees had averaged $1.25 per search, or $18 per hour connected to the NLM computer in Bethesda, Maryland.

AIDSLINE is an online database with more than 90,000 references to AIDS-related journal articles, books, audiovisuals, and conference abstracts.

AIDSTRIALS, produced as a joint effort with NIH's National Institute of Allergy and Infectious Diseases and the Food and Drug Administration, contains current information about more than 500 clinical trials of drugs and vaccines that have been and are being tested by NIH and by private organizations.

AIDSDRUGS contains detailed information about the 190 agents being tested in the clinical trials.

DIRLINE (Directory of Information Resources Online) is an on-line listing of 15,000 organizations and information services that provide information to the public about the National Library of Medicine (a part of the National Institutes of Health), which is the world's largest library of the health sciences. The NLM Board of Regents, the official body of appointed advisors, meets three times a year to consider matters of policy affecting the Library and the public health.

Free access for members.

AIDS-STAT
Access: E-mail
All requests to be added to or deleted from this distribution list, problems, questions, etc., should be sent to: AIDS-STAT-REQUEST@WUBIOS.WUSTL.EDU

A discussion list for the distribution of AIDS statistics from various agencies. The prime information being distributed will be the Center for Disease Control's monthly *AIDS Surveillance Report*.
Owner: David Dodell
DDODELL@STJHMC.FIDONET.ORG

AIDS_INTL
Access: E-mail
LISTSERV@RUTVM1
LISTSERV@RUTGERS.EDU

A discussion list for the International Committee for Electronic Communication on AIDS (ICECA). The purpose of ICECA is to foster international coordination of electronic activities on AIDS. It also tries to assist interested individuals and organizations to participate electronically and to identify and arrange activities.
Owner: Michael Smith
MNSMITH@UMAECS

AIDSNEWS
Access: E-mail
LISTSERV@RUTVM1
LISTSERV@RUTGERS.EDU

The AIDSNews Forum is used for the discussion of any issue relating to AIDS/ARC, as well as *AIDS Treatment News* reports on experimental and alternative treatments, especially those available now. It collects information from medical journals and from interviews with scientists, physicians and other health practitioners, and persons with AIDS or ARC; it does not recommend particular therapies, but seeks to increase the options available. The ethical and public policy issues around AIDS treatment research will also be examined. *AIDS Treatment News, Northern Lights Alternatives*, and many other publications are also distributed to this e-conference.

To protect privacy, the subscriber e-conference is kept confidential. If you have any problems subscribing to the e-conference send mail to the Coordinator.

Owner: Michael Smith
MSMITH@UMAECS

CHAT (AIDS DATABASE)

Access: Telnet
telnet://debra.doc.ca or telnet://192.16.212.15
Login: **CHAT**

CHAT (Conversational Hypertext Access Technology) is a natural language information system. This information retrieval technology was developed by Industry Canada. Please note that your interactions with CHAT are being recorded. You will have a chance to leave comments at the end of your session.

For information about CHAT, download the file */pub/chat/info.page* from DEBRA.DGBT.DOC.CA using anonymous FTP, or contact:

Thom Whalen
Phone: (613) 990-4683
THOM@DEBRA.DGBT.DOC.CA
Andrew Patrick
Phone: (613) 990-4675
ANDREW@DEBRA.DGBT.DOC.CA

HIVNET (GLOBAL ELECTRONIC NETWORK FOR AIDS, EUROPE)

Access: Gopher
gopher://gopher.hivnet.org:70

Excellent AIDS information source. Huge collection of documents.

ICECA
Access: E-mail
ICECA@RUTVM1

Subscription to this list is limited to committee members. Mail may be sent to the committee by anyone. Further information about ICECA may be obtained from the list owner.

International Committee for Electronic Communication on AIDS (ICECA). The purpose of ICECA:

- To foster international coordination of electronic activities on AIDS.
- To assist interested individuals and organizations to participate electronically.
- To identify and arrange activities.

Owner: Michael Smith
MNSMITH@UMAECS

NIAID (NATIONAL INSTITUTE OF ALLERGY AND INFECTIOUS DISEASE) GOPHER SERVER

Access: Gopher
gopher://odie.niaid.nih.gov/11

The NIAID Gopher provides a wide variety of information appealing to both the researcher and the administrator. It has links to the most up-to-date information resources, concentrating on research and reference tools. Of special interest is the AIDS INFORMATION directory, which contains NIAID Press Releases, Center for Disease Control Daily AIDS Summaries, NIAID Protocol Recruitment Sheets, and many more items of an AIDS/HIV nature.

Contributions are welcomed.

Owner: Derrick White
CDW@NIAID.NIH.GOV
Phone: (301) 402-0980 x 424

SCI.MED.AIDS

Access: Usenet

AIDS: treatment, pathology/biology, HIV prevention discussion group.

SOUTHEAST FLORIDA AIDS INFORMATION NETWORK

Access: Telnet
telnet://callcat.med.miami.edu or telnet://129.171.78.1
Login: **LIBRARY**
Select **L** on main menu
Select **1** on next menu
SEFAIN Database

Users may search for AIDS Information by any of the following:

PERSON/ORG/RESEARCH
Organization TYPE
MEDICAL Specialty
Research SITE
Research TYPE
Res ELIGIBILITY
HEALTH&SOCIAL Serv
Mental HEALTH Serv
EDUC & Info Serv

This project is sponsored in part by the National Library of Medicine.

WU-AIDS

Access: Usenet
Sci.Med.AIDS Newsgroup

Owner: Michael Smith
MNSMITH@UMAECS
WUVMD

AMYOTROPHIC LATERAL SCLEROSIS

ALS
Access: E-mail

A discussion list for those interested in Amyotrophic Lateral Sclerosis (ALS), or Lou Gehrig's Disease. This list has been set up to serve the worldwide ALS community. That is, ALS patients, ALS support/discussion groups, ALS clinics, ALS researchers, etc. Others are welcome (and invited) to join. THIS IS NOT A LISTSERV SETUP. For more information, please send e-mail to BRO@HUEY.MET.FSU.EDU (Bob Broedel).

ALS DIGEST

Access: E-mail
To subscribe, unsubscribe, or to contribute notes, send e-mail to BRO@HUEY.MET.FSU.EDU (Bob Broedel)

This publication covers all aspects of Amyotrophic Lateral Sclerosis (ALS), or Lou Gehrig's Disease. This includes ALS patients, patient supporters, physicians, support groups, research centers, etc.
Owner: Bob Broedel
BRO@HUEY.MET.FSU.EDU

ARTHRITIS

ALT.SUPPORT.ARTHRITIS

Access: Usenet

A discussion of issues concerning arthritis sufferers.

ALZHEIMER DISEASE

ALZHEIMER NETWORK/DISCUSSION GROUP

Access: E-mail
MAJORDOMO@WUBIOS.WUSTL.EDU
In the BODY of the message, send the command: **subscribe ALZHEIMER** (no name necessary)

ALZHEIMER is an e-mail discussion group for patients, professional and family caregivers, researchers, public policy makers, students, and anyone with an interest in Alzheimer's or related dementing disorders in older adults.

ALZHEIMER is intended to provide interested individuals from various perspectives an opportunity to share questions, answers, suggestions, and tips.

Contact: ALZHEIMER-OWNER@WUBIOS.WUSTL.EDU
Washington University School of Medicine
Alzheimer's Disease Research Center
660 South Euclid Ave, Campus Box 8111-ADRC
Saint Louis, MO 63110-1093
Phone: (314) 362-2881
FAX: (314) 362-4763

ALZHEIMER WEB

Access: World Wide Web
http://werple.mira.net.au/~dhs/ad.html

A resource for Alzheimer's disease researchers and for the people who have an interest in research developments. The home page includes news, articles, and conference reports.

Contact: David Small
DAVID_SMALL@MUWAYF.UNIMELB.EDU.AU

CANCER

ASTRA

Access: See description for accessing from various computer systems.

An access system for databases distributed on EARN/BITNET. The ASTRA service maintains multiple databases called *META databases*. Each one has an abstract containing information about the contents, i.e., title, name of the authors, a brief description of the database, the main arguments dealt with in the database, and the language. Of interest to those in the health sciences is the ONCO database.
ONCO database

This bibliographic list keeps track of the work concerning ongoing research related to the Oncology field in Italy. The list includes work from different research groups at various institutions. The language is English.
NETWORK ACCESS AND USAGE

The ASTRA database is accessible by EARN/BITNET and non-EARN/BITNET users. For EARN/BITNET users, user interfaces for IBM VM/CMS and DEC VAX/VMS are developed. A batch language format has also been developed for non-EARN/BITNET users and users of different operation systems.

To access the ASTRA system the EARN/BITNET users must have the user interface on their disk. The user interface can be obtained from:
ASTRADB@ICNUCEVM with the following commands:

For IBM VM/CMS **GET ASTRA EXEC**
For DEC VAX/VMS **GET ASTRA PAS**

After the files are received and stored on the disk, the server is accessed by entering:

For IBM VM/CMS **ASTRA**
For DEC VAX/VMS **RUN ASTRA**

Detailed information on the system can be retrieved by getting the file *ASTRA INFO* from ASTRADB@ICNUCEVM.

BRAINTMR
Access: E-mail
LISTSERV@MITVMA.MIT.EDU

A forum to discuss topics related to all types of brain tumors whether benign or malignant. Information and experiences are shared among patients, their supporters, all kinds of medical professionals, and researchers who study brain tumor growth/treatment.

Owner: Samantha Scolamiero
SAMAJANE@ATHENA.MIT.EDU
Brain Tumor Survivor (cpa/brainstem epidermoid)
182 Redington Street
Swampscott, MA 01907-2135
Home Phone: (617) 593-5095
SAMAJANE@ATHENA.MIT.EDU

BREAST-CANCER
Access: E-mail

LISTSERV@MORGAN.UCS.MUN.CA

An open discussion list for any issue relating to breast cancer. This is an unmoderated list open to researchers, physicians, patients, family, and friends of patients for the discussion of any issue relating to breast cancer.

While some of the list will be devoted to discussions of medical advances, as well as possible therapeutic treatments, both mainstream and alternative, the list should also have a less rigorous side to it. The list does not recommend particular therapies but seeks to increase the information available on options.

Owner: J. Church, Ph.D
Terry Fox Cancer Research Labs
Faculty of Medicine
Memorial University of Newfoundland

THE BREAST CANCER INFORMATION CLEARINGHOUSE
Access: Gopher
gopher://nysernet.org:70/11/BCIC

THE BREAST CANCER INFORMATION CLEARINGHOUSE is an Internet-accessible resource for breast cancer patients and their families. Through funding provided by New York State, NYSERNet will establish partnerships with the many organizations which provide information and services to the public. Information currently accessible includes patient education materials from the American Cancer Society and the National Cancer Institute, statistical information compiled by the New York State Department of Health, lists of ACR-accredited mammography facilities in New York State, listings of support groups around the country, many informative articles from the National Alliance of Breast Cancer Organization's newsletter, and relevant state and federal legislation relating to breast cancer.

Contact: TMDAMON@NYSERNET.ORG

CANCER-L
Access: E-mail
LISTSERV@WVNVM

This list is a public list for the discussion of cancer-related topics.

Owner: Susan Rodman
U0AC3@WVNVM

CANCERNET

Access: E-mail; Gopher; World Wide Web

See description below for detailed access information.

CancerNet is a quick and easy way to obtain, through E-mail, cancer information from the National Cancer Institute (NCI). CancerNet lets you request statements from the NCI's Physician Data Query (PDQ) database, fact sheets on various cancer topics from the NCI's Office of Cancer Communications, and citations and abstracts on selected topics from the CANCERLIT database. Selected information is available in Spanish.

The CancerNet Contents List changes at the beginning of each month as new statements and other information is added. CancerNet is accessed through a number of different networks including BITNET and Internet. There is no charge for the service unless your local computer center charges for use of e-mail.

To access CancerNet send e-mail to:
CANCERNET@ICICC.NCI.NIH.GOV

In the body of the message enter **HELP** to receive the instructions and most current contents list. If you have the contents list and would like to receive a particular statement or piece of information enter the code from the Contents List. If you want more than one piece of information enter the relevant code on a separate line.

The information in CancerNet is also available on Gopher (gopher.nih.gov), and the NCI's International Cancer Information Center World Wide Web server (http://www.icic.nci.nih.gov).

Contact:
Cheryl Burg
CancerNet Project Manager
National Cancer Institute
9000 Rockville Pike, Bldg 82, Rm 103A
Bethesda, MD 20892
Phone: 301-496-8880
Fax: 301-480-8105
CHERYL@ICICC.NCI.NIH.GOV

TALARIA

Access: World Wide Web, Telnet
http://www.stat.washington.edu/TALARIA/TALARIA.html

telnet://txcancer.mda.uth.tmc.edu or telnet://129.106.60.97
User Name: TCDC

Hypermedia Clinical Practice Guidelines for Cancer Pain, Talaria is a hypermedia World Wide Web implementation of the AHCPR Guidelines on Cancer Pain. Hypertext-linked section headings include: Overview, Assessment of Pain in the Patient with Cancer, Pharmacologic Management, Nonpharmalogic Management: Physical and Psychosocial, Nonpharmalogic Management: Invasive Therapies, Procedure-related Pain in Adults and Children, Pain in Special Populations, Monitoring the Quality of Pain Management Texas Cancer Data Center. The Texas Cancer Data Center is funded by the Texas Cancer Council as a component of the Texas Cancer Plan to provide computerized information on cancer demographics, resources, services, and programs to all who plan, develop, fund, provide, need, and/or use cancer resources in Texas.

CHRONIC FATIGUE SYNDROME

CFS-L

Access: E-mail
LISTSERV@NIHLIST
LISTSERV@LIST.NIH.GOV

This list concerns Chronic Fatigue Syndrome. The discussions seek to serve the needs of persons with chronic fatigue syndrome by enabling a broad range of CFS-related topics. Subscription is open and the list is unmoderated. Please note that any advice which may be given on this list regarding diagnoses or treatments, etc., reflects only the opinion of the individual posting the message; people with CFS ought to consult with a licensed health care practitioner who is familiar with the syndrome.

Owner: Roger Burns
BITNET: BFU@NIHCU.BITNET
Internet: RBURNS@CAP.GWU.EDU
Compuserv: 73260.1014@COMPUSERVE.COM
Genie: R.BURNS34@GENIE.GEIS.COM

CFS-MED

Access: E-mail
LISTSERV@NIHLIST

Chronic Fatigue Syndrome/CFIDS medical list.

CFS-NEWS

Access: E-mail
LISTSERV@NIHLIST
LISTSERV@LIST.NIH.GOV

The CFS-NEWS electronic newsletter focuses on medical news about CFS/CFIDS/ME and is issued at least once each month. It is based at the NIH-LIST Listserv.

CFS-NEWS (CHRONIC FATIGUE SYNDROME NEWSLETTER CFIDS/ME)

Access: E-mail
LISTSERV@NIHLIST
LISTSERV@LIST.NIH.GOV

This independent newsletter seeks to serve the CFS community by quickly disseminating information about current medical research on CFS. It will be issued about once each month to give updates on these developments. Other CFS topics of interest to the readership will also be covered. Advice and contributions of news items are welcome.

Archives of CFS-NEWS back issues can be listed by sending the command **INDEX CFS-NEWS** to:

LISTSERV@NIHLIST or to LISTSERV@LIST.NIH.GOV

CFS-WIRE

Access: E-mail
LISTSERV@SJUVM
LISTSERV@SJUVM.STJOHNS.EDU

The CFS-WIRE list is where support groups exchange newsletter articles and other news. Subscription is open to all, although support group representatives need to register to be able to post messages. Registration information is sent with the general subscription.

CFS/CFIDS/ME RESOURCES

Access: E-mail

LISTSERV@SJUVM
LISTSERV@SJUVM.STJOHNS.EDU

Please note the other Internet resources that focus on CFS/CFIDS/ME Resources on this Listserv and elsewhere. Resources include: a file database; a Newswire service for support groups; an electronic newsletter (focusing on medical research); and a general discussion group where advice and information are exchanged among patients each day.

The CFS-FILE list hosts a wide variety of files containing medical journal articles, information on related health issues, advice on coping, social security, related illnesses (candida, Lyme disease, etc.) and others.

To retrieve specific files, note the filenames on the FILELIST and then send the command **GET <filename1> <filename2>** to the LISTSERV address (each file has a two-part name).

Also, there is a comprehensive list of electronic and other resources that all patients should review, contained in the file *CFS-RES.TXT* available at either Listserv.

For electronic journals, see CFS-WIRE and CFS-NEWS under the Electronic Publications category.

For a discussion group, see the CFS-L list.
There is a separate CFS file database at a different Listserv in Albany, New York. For information on that database, send commands just as above to the address
LISTSERV%ALBNYDH2.BITNET@ALBANY.EDU or to
LISTSERV@ALBANY.BITNET
Contact:
NIHLIST

CYSTIC FIBROSIS

CYSTIC-L
Access: E-mail
LISTSERV@YALEVM

LISTSERV@YALEVM.CIS.YALE.EDU

The CYSTIC-L discussion group focuses on the holistic impact of cystic fibrosis. While much of the list will be devoted to discussions of new medical advances as well as possible therapeutic and nutritional treatments, the list should also have a less rigorous side to it.

If you forward this on to a list that might like to know about it, please contact the owner, below, to avoid overreproduction. Of course, passing this along to anyone who might be interested is the entire purpose this message is being posted.

Owner: Antony Dugdale
ANTDUGL@MINERVA.CIS.YALE.EDU

MUCO-FR

Access: E-mail
LISTSERV@FRMOP11

Cystic Fibrosis discussion list—France (Mucoviscidoses).

Owner: Michel Jorda
JORDA@FRCISM51
JORDA@FRSUN12

DEVELOPMENTAL DISORDERS

AUTISM

Access: E-mail
LISTSERV@SJUVM

This is a discussion list devoted to the developmentally disabled. Autism's purpose is to provide a forum for those who are developmentally disabled, their teachers, and those interested in this area. The list provides a forum for the understanding and treatment of all types of developmental disability and to further networking among those so handicapped to increase their interaction with the rest of society.

Owner: Bob Zenhausern
DRZ@SJUVM.BITNET

BIFIDA-L

Access: E-mail
LISTSERV@MERCURY.DSU.EDU

BIFIDA-L is for the discussion of any issue relating to spina bifida. This list provides support and information to people with spina bifida as well as parents, siblings, and others.

Owner: Loren Aman
AMANL@COLUMBIA.DSU.EDU

DOWN-SYN

Access: E-mail
LISTSERV@NDSUVM1
LISTSERV@VM1.NODAK.EDU

A mailing list for discussion of Down Syndrome. This mailing list will be gatewayed with the corresponding Usenet newsgroup called BIT.LIST-SERV.DOWN-SYN. The owner is also starting a Fidonet conference, Down-Syn, which will also be gatewayed with this mailing list. This mailing list will be gatewayed with the corresponding Usenet newsgroup, BIT.LISTSERV.DOWN-SYN.

Owner: Bill McGarry
Phone: (203) 926-6187

MOTORDEV

Access: E-mail
LISTSERV@UMDD

Human Motor Skill Development.

DIABETES

DIABETES

Access: E-mail
LISTSERV@IRLEARN

International Research Project on Diabetes.
Owner: Martin Wehlou
WEHLOU@FGEN.RUG.AC.BE

DIABETIC

Access: E-mail
LISTSERV@PCCVM

Open discussion forum for DIABETIC patient concerns. This forum is open to all users on this and any other node to aid diabetic persons in the exchange of views, problems, anxieties, and other aspects of their condition. As this is a public forum, all messages are subject to review by anyone who might request a copy. This list was started in response to comments from some of the users of DIABETES@IRLEARN that perhaps a separate forum for diabetic patient questions and comments could be made available.
Owner: R N Hathhorn
SYSMAINT@PCCVM

DRI NET

Access: Gopher
gopher://drinet.med.miami.edu/1

The Diabetes Research International Network is provided through a gopher from The University of Miami School of Medicine to give Internet access to diabetes research materials and resources.

DISABILITY/HANDICAP

ADA-LAW

Access: E-mail
LISTSERV@NDSUVM1
LISTSERV@VM1.NODAK.EDU

A discussion about any aspect of the Americans with Disabilities Act (ADA) and other disability-related laws.
Owner: WTM@SHELDEV.SHEL.ISC-BR.COM

ASSISTIVE TECHNOLOGY DATABASE INTERFACE

Access: Telnet
telnet://bongo.cc.utexas.edu or telnet://128.83.186.13
Login **tatp**

TATP maintains ATDI as a public database which aids consumers in locating disability assistive equipment and services. ATDI is meant to help create a list of vendors in a certain region who provide certain services. If you have problems using ATDI or questions about it, send e-mail to TATP@BONGO.CC.UTEXAS.EDU with a subject of "ATDI help." Also, any comments, suggestions or new data are welcome.

CORNUCOPIA OF DISABILITY INFORMATION (CODI)

Access: Gopher
gopher://val-dor.cc.buffalo.edu/1

CODI is a gopher intended to serve as a community resource for consumers and professionals by providing via the Internet disability-related information in a wide variety of areas. The information addresses university (SUNY@Buffalo), local (Buffalo & WNY), state, national, and international audiences. Its contents are determined by these communities; their submissions and suggestions are welcome.

Ideally, material should be submitted in computer-readable form. However, printed text is also acceptable if the print quality is sufficient for it to be scanned. (Generally, xerox copies scan poorly.) Often it becomes necessary to rewrite or reformat the material. As a result, errors may appear. Please notify Contact of these so they may be corrected.

Currently, the material is accessible via 22 main menu items. This article, "About the Cornucopia of Disability Information," is the first menu item. Due to the continuous addition of new information, the organization of the menus is bound to change along with their contents. Because of CODI's size and its frequency of change, menu item #2—What's New in Codi—is included for the frequent browser. "What's New" lists modifications, their dates and locations.

Contact: Jay Leavitt
LEAVITT@UBVMSB
LEAVITT@UBVMSB.CC.BUFFALO.EDU

DO-IT INTERNET RESOURCE LIST

Access: Gopher
gopher://hawking.u.washington.edu

With partial funding from the National Science Foundation, the Do-It program has produced a list of mailing lists, newsletters, newsgroups, and gopher sites which contain information of interest to people with disabilities. The list is short, about 23 kb in length, but thorough.

Contact: Dean Martineau
DEAMAR@U.WASHINGTON.EDU

HANDICAP

Access: FTP
ftp://handicap.shel.isc-br.com or ftp://129.189.4.184
Login **anonymous**
Password **Your e-mail address**

This is an anonymous FTP site that contains only disability-related files and/or programs. There are about 40 directories with over 500 files/programs covering all types of disabilities. The Handicap BBS List, a list of 800 BBSs carrying disability-related information, originates here.

THE HANDICAP DIGEST

Access: E-mail
WTM@BUNKER.SHEL.ISC-BR.COM

The HANDICAP DIGEST is an electronic-mail-only digest of articles relating to all types of issues affecting the handicapped. The articles are taken from the Usenet newsgroup, the Handicap News, (see MISC.HANDICAP below) and various Fidonet conferences such as ABED, BlinkTalk, SilentTalk, Chronic Pain, Spinal Injury, Rare Conditions, and several others.

HISTORY AND ANALYSIS OF DISABILITIES NEWSLETTER

Access: E-mail
LISTSERV@SJUVM.STJOHNS.EDU
See subscription information below

History and Analysis of Disabilities Newsletter covers news, conferences, seminars, books, articles, theses, research, organizations, analysis, etc. on his-

tory of disabilities and disabled persons, conceptual analysis of disability issues. Produced two to three times per year. Sponsored by History of Disabilities Network, Centre for Independent Living, Toronto (CILT), and ALTER—
International Society for the History of Disabilities (Paris). Available in paper
copy for $10 (U.S. or Canadian funds) for four issues. Send e-mail to
FCTY7310@RYERSON to request subscription.

Information Technology and Disabilities (ISSN 1073-5127) is a new, quarterly electronic journal devoted to all aspects of computer use by persons
with disabilities. It is intended to fill a void in the professional literature by
bringing together articles by educators (kindergarten through college), librarians, human resources and rehabilitation professionals, as well as campus computing and other professionals concerned with the effective use of
technology by people with all kinds of disabilities. The premier issue of *Information Technology and Disabilities* reflects the breadth of coverage that
the journal's editorial board plans to maintain in future issues. Feature articles include a case study of an accessible CD-ROM workstation at the Seattle Library for the Blind, a profile of the St. John's University UNIBASE
system, including the many rehabilitation resources housed there, and an
article on the Royal Society for the Blind (Australia), which provides excellent screen design principles for enhanced accessibility. Feature articles
are supplemented by news of interest to computer users with disabilities as
well as educators, librarians, rehabilitation and other professionals interested in the uses of new and emerging technologies by people with disabilities. Individual subscriptions are free of charge, and two subscription options are available:

1. Receive ENTIRE ISSUE AUTOMATICALLY. Please note: individual
issues will range from 75 to 150 pages. Address e-mail message to LIST-
SERV@SJUVM.STJOHNS.EDU and leave subject line blank. Send the following one-line message: **sub itd-jnl your name**
2. The journal will be made available at the St. John's University gopher.
To receive each issue's TABLE OF CONTENTS ONLY: address e-mail message to LISTSERV@SJUVM.STJOHNS.EDU and leave subject line blank.
Send the following one-line message: **sub itd-toc your name**

The Table of Contents will provide abstracts of articles as well as explicit
instructions for using the gopher-based version of *Information Technology
and Disabilities*.

Submission of Articles

Information Technology and Disabilities is a peer-reviewed journal. Requests for authors' guidelines should be submitted to:

Tom McNulty
Editor-in-Chief
Bobst Library, New York University
70 Washington Square South
New York, NY 10012
Phone (voice): (212) 998-2519
TDD (leave message): (212) 998-4980
E-mail MCNULTY@ACFCLUSTER.NYU.EDU

LD-LIST

Access: E-mail
LD-LIST-OWNER@EAST.PIMA.EDU
In the BODY of the note say only: **SUBSCRIBE**

Learning Disability Information Exchange List. LD-List is an open, unmoderated, international forum that provides an information exchange network for individuals interested in learning disabilities. Subscribers include persons with learning disabilities, family members and friends, educators and administrators, researchers, and others wishing to know more about this disease. Any topic related to learning disabilities is appropriate for discussion.

MISC.HANDICAP

Access: Usenet

This newsgroup covers all areas of disabilities—technical, medical, educational, legal, etc.

SJU ELECTRONIC REHABILITATION RESOURCE CENTER

Access: Gopher
gopher://sjuvm.stjohns.edu

Two major software archives available through Gopher. The Handicap News BBS Archive and the University of Oakland (Rochester, Michigan) Handicap Archive each contain hundreds of files concerned with all aspects of disabilities and rehabilitation. Both archives can be accessed from the Rehabilitation Resource Center main menu.

FIBROMYALGIA

FIBROM-L

Access: E-mail
LISTSERV@VMD.CSO.UIUC.EDU

FIBROM-L is a discussion forum for the disease/syndrome known as fibromyalgia/fibrositis. It is an opportunity for researchers, physicians, patients, family and friends of patients, and other interested persons to discuss this condition. FIBROM-L is an unmoderated list open to all interested subscribers. It is supported by the Computing and Communications Services Office (CCSO) of the University of Illinois at Urbana-Champaign (UIUC).

Owners:
Sandra Bott
SBOTT@VMD.CSO.UIUC.EDU
Molly Mack
MOLLYM@VMD.CSO.UIUC.EDU

GASTROINTESTINAL DISORDERS

DIARRHOE

Access: E-mail
LISTSERV@SEARN
LISTSERV@SEARN.SUNET.SE

DIARRHOE is a mailing list for information exchange and discussions on all aspects related to diseases, disorders, and chemicals which cause diarrhoea in humans and animals.

IBDlist (INFLAMMATORY BOWEL DISEASE)

Access: E-mail
REQUEST%MVAC23@UDEL.EDU

IBDlist is a moderated mailing list which discusses all aspects of inflammatory bowel diseases, with particular emphasis on Crohn's disease and ulcerative colitis. Anyone with an interest in these diseases, whether direct or indirect, is welcome. This list will also act as a clearinghouse for information and discussion of current treatments, research, and other information related to IBDs. This list is not restricted to those suffering from one of the diseases or directly linked to IBD patients.

Owner: Thomas Lapp

INGEST

Access: E-mail
LISTSERV@CUVMA

Ingestive Disorders Mailing list.

Owners:
Henry Kissileff
HRKOM@CUVMB
Jerry B. Altzman
JAUUS@CUVMB

IMMUNE SYSTEM DISORDERS

IMMUNE

Access: E-mail
LISTSERV@WEBER.UCSD.EDU

This list is a support group for people with immune-system breakdowns (and their symptoms) such as Chronic Fatigue Syndrome, Lupus, Candida, Hypoglycemia, multiple allergies, learning disabilities, etc. and their significant others, medical caretakers, etc. The group is unmoderated and open to anyone anywhere in the world (no arguments about whether or not these disabilities exist).

All requests to be added to or deleted from this e-conference, problems, questions, etc., should be sent to:

IMMUNE-REQUEST@WEBER.UCSD.EDU

Owner: Cyndi Norman
CNORMAN@UCSD.EDU

LYME DISEASE

LYMENET-L

Access: E-mail
LISTSERV@LEHIGH.EDU

Back issues can be obtained via two methods:
Internet users may use anonymous FTP at:
ftp.Lehigh.EDU:/pub/listserv/lymenet-l/Newsletters/x-yy
(where **x** is the volume number and **yy** is the issue number)

Internet and BITNET users may use the listserver by sending it this command:
get LymeNet-L/Newsletters x-yy
(where **x** is the volume number and **yy** is the issue number)

The LymeNet Newsletter is automatically cross-posted to the sci.med Usenet group

The Newsletter is suitable for both scientific and patient communities, as it contains sections for each

The Lyme Disease E-mail Network. Subscribers to LymeNet-L receive The LymeNet Newsletter approximately twice a month. This publication provides readers with the latest research, treatment, and political news about the Lyme disease epidemic.

Owner: Marc Gabriel
Editor-in-Chief
The LymeNet Newsletter
MCG2@LEHIGH.EDU

MENINGITIS

MENINGITIS EPIDEMIC CASE STUDY

Access: E-mail
LISTSERV@FTP.LIV.AC.UK

The Meningitis Epidemic Case Study is a computer-assisted learning module developed with information collected during an epidemic in Africa. The module is user-friendly and users not familiar with computers need only a short introduction to master the skills required.

The module is fully described in:

Cuevas LE, Moody JB, Macfarlane SBJ, Rada R, Ghaoui C. The use of hypertext to demonstrate the methods of investigating an epidemic of meningitis. *Medical Education* 1993:27;91–96.

The authors welcome comments and suggestions concerning both the academic content and the hypertext features of the module. Such comments can be sent by post or e-mail to the address below.

The aims of the module are to familiarize the user with the epidemiology of epidemic bacterial meningitis in Africa and to practise with a real-life problem of diagnosing an epidemic of bacterial meningitis with limited sources of information.

Computer Requirements

The system requires an IBM-compatible PC with at least 540 kb of free RAM, a hard disk with at least 1.5 Mb free space, mouse, and EGA (or better) colour graphics adaptor.

Software

The module was developed using the hypertext software LINKWAY. The release version of the Meningitis Epidemic Case Study uses a special "read-only" module, allowing applications to be freely distributed.

Distribution

epidemic.zip the compressed version of the module
epinst.bat the installation batch file
unzip.exe public domain uncompression software
README background information and installation instructions

An option within the module is to use the public domain epidemiological software Epi-Info to analyse data. Files containing a database of the information collected about the epidemic, in Epi-Info format, are copied to the Epi Info directory—assumed to be *C:\EPI5*

Epi Info is available by FTP from the SIMTEL archives at ftp://oak.oakland.edu and other mirror sites in the *pub/statistics* directory.

Software prepared and distributed by:

The Liverpool Epidemiology Programme
Liverpool School of Tropical Medicine
Pembroke Place
Liverpool L3 5QA
UK

Access: The software is available by anonymous FTP from ftp://ftp.liv.ac.uk in the directory *~ftp/pub/epidemic*. The package is distributed in compressed form together with the uncompression software.

Contact: Mr. J. B. Moody
MT04@LIVERPOOL.AC.UK

MULTIPLE SCLEROSIS

MSLIST-L

Access: E-mail
LISTSERV@NCSUVM

Multiple Sclerosis Discussion/Support.

PARKINSON'S DISEASE

PARKINSN

Access: E-mail
LISTSERV@VM.UTCC.UTORONTO.CA

Parkinson's Disease Information Exchange Network. PARKINSN is an open, unmoderated, international forum that provides an information exchange network for individuals interested in Parkinson's Disease. Subscribers include persons with Parkinson's disease, family members and friends, health care workers, researchers, and others wishing to know more about this disease. Any topic related to Parkinson's disease is appropriate for discussion.

Owner: Barbara Patterson,
PATTERSO@FHS.CSU.MCMASTER.CA

Repetitive Strain Injury

REPETITIVE STRAIN INJURY (RSI) NETWORK NEWSLETTER
Access: E-mail, FTP
Call (703) 237-5130 and request to be put on the mailing list

The RSI Network is a bimonthly newsletter of information for people concerned about carpal tunnel syndrome, tendonitis, and other repetitive strain injuries. It covers software, hardware, publications, ergonomic resources, worker's compensation, legislation, employment services, practitioners, personal stories of RSI sufferers, and more.

FTP Archives
To access a pointer to information on tendonitis, carpal tunnel syndrome, and other repetitive strains, FTP to ftp://sunsite.unc.edu and look at the information in */pub/docs/typing-injury*, especially the RSI Network Newsletter, whose back issues are in the directory */pub/docs/typing-injury/rsi-network.sunsite.unc.edu*

SOREHAND
Access: E-mail
LISTSERV@UCSFVM

Discussion of carpal tunnel syndrome and tendonitis
Owner: Richard Karpinski
OWNER@CCNEXT.UCSF.EDU

Schizophrenia

SCHIZ-L: CLINICAL AND BASIC SCIENCE RESEARCH IN SCHIZOPHRENIA
Access: E-mail
LISTSERV@UMAB.BITNET
LISTSERV@UMAB.UMD.EDU

SCHIZ-L is an unmoderated discussion list devoted to schizophrenia research. The objective of the list is to provide a forum for communications among researchers and others interested in this mental illness. It is hoped that this forum will facilitate discussion of both published and unpublished findings and ideas, foster potential collaborations between investigators, and develop into an information resource for those in this field.

Owner: Steve Daviss
SDAVISS@COSY.AB.UMD.EDU

SCHIZOPH (SCHIZOPHRENIA INFORMATION EXCHANGE NETWORK)

Access: E-mail
LISTSERV@VM.UTCC.UTORONTO.CA

SCHIZOPH is an open, unmoderated, global electronic conference that provides an information exchange network on issues related to schizophrenia. Subscribers include people and organizations interested in or working on issues related to schizophrenia. These include family and friends, researchers, health care providers, support and advocacy groups. Any topic related to schizophrenia is appropriate for discussion. We can use this space to make announcements, share ideas, papers, bibliographies, resources, experiences, etc.

Owner: Chris Glover
CGLOVER@OISE.ON.CA

Sleep Disorders

SLEEP-L

Access: E-mail
LISTSERV@QUCDN

For discussion of sleep disorders. Membership is restricted to health care providers involved in academic or clinical pursuits related to sleep or discussion of sleep disorders.

SNORE CENTRAL

Access: World Wide Web

http://www.access.digex.net/~faust/s/dord

This page includes general information about sleep disorders and sleep disorder-related organizations.

Contact: Doug Linder
FAUST@ACCESS.DIGEX.NET

SPEECH/SIGHT/HEARING DISORDERS

BLIND-L

Access: E-mail
LISTSERV@UAFSYSB

Computer use by and for the sight-impaired discussion list. This list is intended to provide a forum for discussion of computer use by the blind and visually impaired. Topics relating to use of VM/CMS and PCs are of particular interest, but discussion of other systems is also welcome.

Owner: Daniel P. Martin
DMARTIN@UAFSYSB

CDMAJOR

Access: E-mail
LISTSERV@ENTVM

Communication disorder discussion List.

CNET-DIL

Access: E-mail
LISTSERV@ARIZVM

CNET-DIL is for the discussion of diagnostic dilemmas, especially for specialists in speech and hearing. It is maintained by the national center for neurogenic communication disorders.

COMMDIS

Access: E-mail

COMSERV@RPIECS

Speech disorders discussion list. Subscriptions to this list must be sent to: COMSERVE@RPIECS

Send the following command to that address to begin your subscription: **Join Commdis [Your name]**

Owner: SUPPORT@RPITSVM (Comserve Support Staff)

DEAF-L

Access: E-mail
LISTSERV@SIUCVMB

Discussion list for issues concerning the hearing impaired.

Owner: Roy Miller
GE0013@SiUCVMB

DEAFBLND

Access: E-mail
LISTSERV@UKCC

Dual sensory impairment (deaf-blindness) is the topic of this forum. The mission of DEAFBLND is to share information, inquiries, ideas, and opinions on matters pertaining to dual sensory impairment. The list is open to professionals in the field, to individuals with DSI, and to their families and friends.

Owner: Bob Moore
STR002@UKCC

RPLIST

Access: E-mail
LISTSERV@SJUVM.STJOHNS.EDU

The list is intended for retinitis pigmentosa (RP) sufferers, their friends and relatives, and anyone with an interest in RP. RP is used here as a generic name for all retinal degenerations, including, e.g., macular degeneration and Usher's syndrome. Discussions are welcome on any subject relevant to RP, with an emphasis on issues specific to low vision and degenerative vision; issues relevant to blindness in general are better kept on existing blindness-related lists and newsgroups. Medical aspects of RP are also of interest, but are not the main focus of the list.

Owners:
Nicolas Graner
RPLIST-REQUEST@LRI.FR
Roger Myers
MYERS@AB.WVNET.EDU

STUTT-L

Access: E-mail
LISTSERV@TEMPLEVM

Stuttering: Research and Clinical Practice Mailing list to facilitate the exchange of information among researchers and clinicians working on the problem of stuttering. Researchers are encouraged to submit descriptions of current projects (purpose, procedures, results if any, current status) and to raise questions that may be of interest to other researchers. Clinicians are encouraged to describe unusual cases.

Owner: Woody Starkweather
V5002E@TEMPLEVM

STROKE

STROKE-L

Access: E-mail
LISTSERV@UKCC
LISTSERV@UKCC.UKY.EDU

CerebroVascular Accident. The purpose of the Stroke Lists is to share information and opinions, ideas and inquiries that relate to the topic of stroke.

Owner: Bob Moore
STR002@UKCC.UKY.EDU

MEDICAL SPECIALTIES

ANATOMY

INTERACTIVE ANATOMY PROGRAMS
Access: FTP
ftp://ftp.monash.edu.au
Directory *pub/medical*

Interactive anatomy. All of the series are posted to this site. Make sure to read the *INDEX* file for information on each program.

Owner: Andrei Cornoiu
CORNOIU@MONU1.CC.MONASH.EDU.AU

ANESTHESIOLOGY

ANEST-L
Access: E-mail
LISTSERV@UBVM
LISTSERV@UBVM.CC.BUFFALO.EDU

This list is a vehicle for the discussion of topics related to anesthesiology and collection of any information related to anesthesiology.

Owner: Andrew M. Sopchak
SOPCHAKA@SNYSYRV1

ANESTHESIA AND CRITICAL CARE RESOURCES ON THE INTERNET
Access: Contact the owner

Specialty list of Anesthesia and Critical Care Resources.

Owner: A.J. Wright, MLS Department of Anesthesiology Library
School of Medicine
University of Alabama at Birmingham
619 19th Street South, JT965
Birmingham, AL 35233-6810

Phone: (205) 934-6500
FAX: (205) 975-5963
MEDS002@UABDPO.DPO.UAB.EDU

ANESTHESIOLOGY ARCHIVES

Access: FTP
ftp://gasnet.med.yale.edu

The archive site for Anesthesiology contains files and programs of interest to anesthesiologists. Files include the complete bibliography of the Society for Neurosurgical Anesthesiology and Critical Care and a neuroanesthesia manual.

The name of the list is ANESTHESIOLOGY@GASNET.MED.YALE.EDU. To subscribe, send e-mail containing the phrase, **subscribe anesthesiology**, to LISTPROC@GASNET.MED.YALE.EDU.

Contact:
Keith J Ruskin, MD
GASNet Administrator
Assistant Professor of Anesthesiology
Yale University School of Medicine
New Haven, CT
Phone: (203) 785-2802
Fax: (203) 785 6664
RUSKIN@GASNET.MED.YALE.EDU

ANESTHESIOLOGY INTERNET GOPHER

Access: Gopher
gopher://eja.anes.hscsyr.edu

Contains information of interest to those interested in the fields of anesthesiology and critical care. Includes bibliographic information, position announcements, lecture notes, case studies, and research abstracts. This Gopher also houses the archives of ANEST-L Listserv list. Messages and updates to the Gopher are announced on the ANEST-L mailing list.

Subscribe to ANEST-L by sending an e-mail message to:

LISTSERV@UBVM.CC.BUFFALO.EDU with the line: **SUBSCRIBE ANEST-L**

Contact: Andrew M. Sopchak, MD
State University of New York

Health Science Center at Syracuse
Department of Anesthesiology
750 East Adams Street
Syracuse, NY 13210
GOPHER@EJA.ANES.HSCSYR.EDU.

GASNET

Access: World Wide Web; Gopher
http://gasnet.med.yale.edu
gopher://gasnet.med.yale.edu

GASNet is a global anesthesiology server network that includes a multimedia textbook, Educational Synopses in Anesthesiology and Critical Care Medicine—the first electronic journal of anesthesiology—and abstracts from several journals, commercial software demonstrations, an e-mail directory as well as links to many other anesthesiology resources on the Internet.

Contact:
Keith J Ruskin, MD
GASNet Administrator
Assistant Professor of Anesthesiology
Yale University School of Medicine
New Haven, CT
Phone: (203) 785-2802
Fax: (203) 785-6664
RUSKIN@GASNET.MED.YALE.EDU

CARDIOLOGY

CARDIAC-PREV

Access: E-mail
MAILSERV@AC.DAL.CA

The Cardiac Prevention Research Centre was created through collaboration between Dalhousie University and Marion Merrell Dow (Canada) Inc. Its goals are to promote research into and communication about the non-pharmacological prevention of coronary heart disease. This mail list is to help fulfil the communication goal. The mail list is not moderated and open to any discussion and questions about prevention of coronary heart disease that does not involve medications. Diet, exercise, and smoking are obvious subjects for discussion, but we should not forget economic, social, educational, and cultural factors.

VANDERBILT ATHEROSCLEROSIS & DISEASES OF THE AORTA

Access: World Wide Web
http://virgil.mc.vanderbilt.edu/Virgil_Lessons/Atherosclerosis/Atherosclerosis.html

This is a multimedia course that reviews the pathogenesis of atherosclerotic lesions.

COMPLEMENTARY/ALTERNATIVE MEDICINE

NATURAL HEALTH SERVICES AVAILABLE ON INTERNET

Access: World Wide Web
http://www.teleport.com:80/~amrta

AMRTA, a pioneering organization that two years ago released the most comprehensive database software package available in the natural medicine field, has just opened three new health information services on Internet. The medical research and teaching organization now offers two home pages on the World Wide Web providing a broad array of information on natural medicine for both general and professional audiences. In addition, a new mailing list opens a fresh forum for discussion among health professionals.

Natural Medicine, Complementary Health Care, and Alternative Therapies

The first Web site, Natural Medicine, Complementary Health Care and Alternative Therapies, is a place to access health information as well as reference health organizations, medical institutions and other health resources available on Internet. The site's Internet address is:

http://www.teleport.com:80/~amrta

Interactive BodyMind Information System

The second Web site provides introductory information on the pioneering AMRTA software program, IBIS, the Interactive BodyMind Information System. That Internet home page can be reached at:

http://www.teleport.com:80/~ibis

IBIS is published by GAIA Multimedia Inc. U.S. sales information is available toll free at (800) 627-6851 weekdays 9 a.m.–5 p.m. Pacific Standard Time. E-mail for IBIS: IBIS@TELEPORT.COM.

Paracelsus

A third new service, PARACELSUS, is a mailing list aimed at promoting communication, collaboration and exploration among health care professionals. Subscription is limited to practitioners, educators, researchers, and students in alternative and conventional medical fields. The list is intended to focus on interesting cases, practical clinical pearls, recent publications, useful anecdotes, and medical news.

Those wishing to participate in PARACELSUS should send an e-mail message to:

MAJORDOMO@TELEPORT.COM reading **SUBSCRIBE PARACELSUS**

As part of the subscription approval process, send a biographical note indicating training, practice and interests to:

PARACELSUS@TELEPORT.COM
E-mail for AMRTA is AMRTA@TELEPORT.COM

Contact: Ella Roggow or Mitchell Stargrove
Phone: (503) 228-6851

DERMATOLOGY

DERM-L

Access: E-mail
LISTSERV@YALEVM
LISTSERV@YALEVM.CIS.YALE.EDU

DERM-L is a mailing list for discussion of topics in the field of dermatology. It is a moderated list that is open to physicians who practice dermatology.

Owner: Robert Langdon
RLANGDON@BIOMED.MED.YALE.EDU

DERMATOLOGY GRAND ROUNDS
Access: World Wide Web

http://netaxis.com/rdrugge/jan95.html

Updated monthly, these dermatologic cases are supported by participants of the Derm-L mailing list.

Contact: Rhett J. Drugge, MD
RDRUGGE@NETAXIS.COM

Emergency Medicine

EMED-L

Access: E-mail
MAJORDOMO@ITSA.UCSF.EDU

For health care professionals in emergency medicine, this list functions as an automatic mail/distribution system for the exchange of information and issues relating to a particular subject—in this case, emergency medicine. As a member of the list you will be able to pose questions or opinions that will automatically be distributed to all other members of the list. As the list grows, you will be able to communicate with members throughout the country—if not the world. This list is sponsored by the Emergency Medicine group at UCSF.

Moderator: Chris Barton
CBARTON@ITSA.UCSF.EDU

EMERGENCY MEDICINE WWW

Access: World Wide Web
http://www.njnet.com/embbs/home.html

This Web page includes clinical photographs, radiographs, emergency medicine job listings, an EM residents clinical case competition, and clinical reviews in pediatric EM, toxicology, and travel medicine.

Contact: Ash Nashed, MD
ASHRAFN@AOL.COM

EMSNY-L

Access: E-mail
LISTSERV@MARIST

Emergency Medical Services is a list devoted to discussion of emergency medical services issues of concern to providers in New York State and elsewhere. Queries will be answered by knowledgeable field providers. Where appropriate, state EMS staff will respond. Files available include the state BLS protocols, the rules and regulations, DNR (do not resuscitate) regulations and policy statement, and hospital emergency department regulation.

Owner: Mike Gilbertson
MEG04@ALBNYDH2ALBNYDH2

HELPNETNetwork Emergency Response Planning.

INJURY-L

Access: E-mail
LISTSERV@WVNVM
LISTSERV@WVNVM.WVNET.EDU

The Center for Rural Emergency Medicine and the Injury Control Center of West Virginia University have established a discussion list on the Internet for injury research, epidemiology, intervention, prevention, and other related issues. The list is open to all persons who share these interests.

Owner: Paul M. (Mike) Furbee
Research Coordinator
Center for Rural Emergency Medicine
P.O. Box 9151
Robert C. Byrd Health Sciences Center
Morgantown, WV 26506
Phone: (304) 293-6682
FURBEE@WVNVM.WVNET.EDU

MISC.EMERG-SERVICES

Access: Usenet

Emergency services discussion group

ENDOCRINOLOGY

REPRENDO
Access: E-mail
LISTSERV@UMAB.UMD.EDU

A mailing list for medical professionals interested in reproductive endocrinology.

EPIDEMIOLOGY

COMPREHENSIVE EPIDEMIOLOGICAL DATA RESOURCE (CEDR)
Access: Gopher
gopher://cedr.lbl.gov/11/

Information includes:
The CEDR Catalog: Introduction
The CEDR Catalog: Overview of CEDR Data
The CEDR Catalog: Becoming an Authorized CEDR Data User
The CEDR Catalog: Methods of Accessing CEDR Data
The CEDR Catalog: Individual CEDR Data File Sets
Experimental CEDR Services
Non-CEDR Information Services Around the World

FORENSIC MEDICINE

FORENS-L
Access: E-mail
LISTSERV@FAUVAX
LISTSERV@ACC.FAU.EDU

Forens-L is an unmoderated discussion list dealing with forensic aspects of anthropology, biology, chemistry, odontology, pathology, psychology, serology, toxicology, criminalistic and expert witnessing, and presentation of evidence in court.

Owner: M. Yasar Iscan
ISCAN@FAUVAX

FORENSIC
Access: E-mail
LISTSERV@UNMVMA

Forensic medicine, anthropology, death investigation, mortality statistics, accident and safety research discussion list.

Owner: David Broudy
DBROUDY@UNMB

GASTROENTEROLOGY

COLUMBIA UNIVERSITY GASTROENTEROLOGY WEB
Access: World Wide Web
http://cpmcnet.columbia.edu/dept/gi/

A good starting point to link to other gastroenterology and liver disease information on the Internet. Planned is a gastroenterology manual for physicians and medical students prepared by the Columbia faculty.

Contact: HJW14@COLUMBIA.EDU

NIDDK (NATIONAL INSTITUTE OF DIABETES AND DIGESTIVE AND KIDNEY DISEASE)
Access: World Wide Web
http://www.niddk.nih.gov/

Includes news releases, patient information services, and links to other related Internet sites.

Contact: Walter W Stewart
STEWART@HELIX.NIH.GOV

General Practice/Community Medicine

CLIN-DX-L
Access: E-mail
MAILSERV@UTHSHCSA.EDU

CLIN-DX-L is for people interested in the teaching and research of the medical physical exam and clinical evaluation. The group is by the Physical Diagnosis Interest Group of the Society of General Internal Medicine. It is unmoderated and open to anyone who is interested.

Contact: Bob Badgett, MD
BADGETT%SHIRE@UTHSCSA.EDU

COMMUNITY HEALTH RESEARCH UNIT DISCUSSION GROUPS
Access: E-mail
LISTSERV@ZEUS.MED.UOTTAWA.CA

The Community Health Research Unit, a system-linked research unit in Ottawa, Canada announces the availability of four e-mail discussion groups which are based on a LISTSERV-like program. This program redirects e-mail to subscribed participants. Four discussion groups have been set up. These include discussion groups on behaviour change strategies, fall prevention in the elderly, community mobilization/development, and general community health issues.

FAMILY-L
Access: E-mail
LISTSERV@MIZZOU1

Academic family medicine discussion.

Owner: Joe Stanford
FCMJOE@MIZZOU1

GENERAL PRACTICE ON-LINE
Access: World Wide Web

http://www.cityscape.co.uk/users/ad88/gp.htm

This site has peer-reviewed articles for primary care providers.

GERONTOLOGY/GERIATRICS

AGEING
Access: E-mail
LISTSERV@DARESBURY.AC.UKGERINET

Aging electronic conference.

GERINET
Access: E-mail
LISTSERV@UBVM
LISTSERV@UBVM.CC.BUFFALO.EDU

Geriatric Health Care Discussion Group. This is a mailing list of those in-terested in geriatric health care. It is intended to have multidisciplinary rep-resentation (e.g., physicians, nurses, social workers, physical therapists, oc-cupational therapists, psychologists, speech therapists, lawyers, nursing home administrators, etc.) of individuals concerned about the well-being of elders.
Owner: Robert S. Stall, MD
DRSTALL@UBVMS.CC.BUFFALO.EDU

EDUHUMAGE-L
Access: E-mail
LISTSERV@ASUACAD

Humanistic Effects of Aging.

LTCARE-L
Access: E-mail
LISTSERV@NIHLIST

This interest group seeks to identify, share, and discuss research findings relevant to public policy on disability (both physical and cognitive), aging, and long-term care. The group is interested in the characteristics of long-term care systems, including eligibility for services, participation rates, socioeconomic status of participants, organizational and financial arrangements, service use, and costs. An area of major emphasis is how changes in public policy would affect programs (e.g., Medicare, Medicaid, Older Americans Act) benefiting frail elderly and other experience of states in the U.S. and other nations in providing long-term care are welcomed. This list is maintained in the office of the Assistant Secretary for Planning and Evaluation (ASPE) located in the U.S. Department of Health and Human Services (DHHS).

Owner: Robert Clark
BOBC@OSASPE.SSW.DHHS.GOV

NIATRN-L

Access: E-mail
LISTSERV@BROWNVM

National Institute of Aging Population Researchers and Trainees List. Involves people performing research on aging and the aged.

Owners:
James McNally
ST403145@BROWNVM
Rose Li
LI%NIA-GW%NIH@NIH3PLUS

SENIOR

Access: E-mail
LISTSERV@INDYCMS

Senior health and living discussion group. Senior is dedicated to the discussion of all issues relating to the health and lives of senior citizens. It is intended to serve in part as a networking tool to facilitate enhancement of senior health and life by matching senior citizen needs with existing services. Senior is open to all persons interested in the health and lives of senior citizens, including health care providers, social service providers, gerontologists, and others.

Owner: John B Harlan
IJBH200@INDYVAX.IUPUI.EDU

INFECTIOUS DISEASE/IMMUNOLOGY

IMMNET-L

Access: E-mail
LISTSERV@DARTCMS1
LISTSERV@DARTCMS1.DARTMOUTH.EDU

Medical Immunization Tracking systems. IMMNET-L is an electronic bulletin board service designed to facilitate a national discussion about immunization tracking systems. State and local health agencies are specifically invited to participate. The purpose is agencies sharing experiences in system design and implementation and is intended to encourage the development of standards for coding and data exchange. Other possible discussion topics could include algorithms for evaluation of compliance and reviews of commercial software.

Contact: James E. Levin, MD, PhD
JLEVIN@UMNHCS.BITNET
JLEVIN@SIMVAX.LABMED.UMN.EDU

IMMUNIZATION ACTION COALITION

Access: World Wide Web
URL http://www.winternet.com/~immunize

Immunization Action Coalition, a 501(c)3 nonprofit organization, works to boost immunization rates in the U.S. The Coalition promotes physician, community, and family awareness of and responsibility for appropriate immunization of all people of all ages against all vaccine-preventable diseases. The Coalition's WWW home page will provide people with electronic versions of their newsletters, Needle Tips and Hepatitis B Coalition News, as well as provide a mailing address to their organization on the Internet.

IMMUNIZATION TRACKING

Access: FTP
ftp://dorothy.cis.unf.edu or ftp://139.62.200.6
Directory *pub/immunization*

Anonymous FTP directory for immunization tracking

PROMED
Access: E-mail
PROMED-REQUEST@USA.HEALTHNET.ORG

ProMED—the Program for Monitoring Emerging Diseases—was set up to establish a direct partnership among scientists concerned with emerging infectious diseases in all parts of the world; building the appropriate networks to encourage communicating and sharing information is a key objective. Reporting of incidents or outbreaks, infectious disease problems of emerging interest, and discussions on how to improve surveillance and response capabilities (including needs at the local level) are especially encouraged. ProMED is a moderated, electronic conference.

Contact: Dr. Stephen S. Morse
Chair, ProMED
The Rockefeller University
1230 York Avenue, Box 120
MORSE@ROCKVAX.ROCKEFELLER.EDU

TRAVEL GOPHER
Access: Gopher
gopher://gopher.moon.com:7000/11h/travel.health

Provides comprehensive information and description of medications and vaccines for world travelers.
Contact: PAUL@GAC.EDU

TULANE TROPICAL MEDICINE WEB PAGE
Access: World Wide Web
http://www.tropmed.tulane.edu

This site includes scientific research projects, U.S. and international academic degree programs, and information on malaria research, disease epidemiology, and chloroquine drug resistance.

MENTAL HEALTH

ALCOHOL
Access: E-mail
LISTSERV@MUACAD

This is an alcohol and drug studies discussion group. ALCOHOL is a unique e-conference offering the BITNET Community a chance to voice their opinions about the abuse of alcohol, illegal and other commonly abused drugs. The e-conference is open to anyone, but contributions from the psychological and medical professions are encouraged. Students are especially encouraged, as they may provide some fresh insight.
Owner: Phillip Charles Oliff
FXX1@LMUACAD

ALCOHOLISM RESEARCH DATABASE
Access: Telnet
telnet://lib.dartmouth.edu
Login **SELECT FILE CORK**

Project CORK collection on alcoholism and substance abuse on the Dartmouth College Library Online System.

APASD-L
Access: E-mail
LISTSERV@VTVM2

APA Research Psychology Network. The APA Science Directorate Funding Bulletin is designed to alert subscribers to research and training funding sources for psychology.
Owners:
Deborah Segal
APASDDES@GWUVM
Cheri Fullerton
APASDCF@GWUVM

DARTMOUTH UNIVERSITY DARTMOUTH MEDICAL SCHOOL DATABASES

Access: Telnet
telnet://lib.dartmouth.edu
1. Type your terminal type
2. Type the command **SELECT FILE** *[name]*, e.g., **SELECT FILE** *CATA-LOG*, **SELECT FILE** *PILOTS*, **SELECT FILE** *CORK*

This system also contains two databases of interest; the *PILOTS* file, an index of literature on posttraumatic stress, and Project *CORK* file, which indexes materials on alcohol and substance abuse.

To exit: **BYE**

LEGALTEN

Access: E-mail
MAJORDOMO@WORLD.STD.COM

The Evaluation Center @ HSRI has set up an Internet Listserv to facilitate assessment of the impacts of interventions in the broad area of interface between the mental health system, the criminal justice system, and the courts. The Network's domain includes such diverse areas as evaluation of the effects of litigation directed toward mental health service system reform, changes in the delivery of mental health services to persons in the custody of the criminal justice system, and the effects of reform in specific areas of mental health law, such as changes in civil commitment criteria, implementation or revision of outpatient commitment statutes and practices, and changes in the insanity defense.

This mailing list is part of The Evaluation Center's Topical Evaluation Network on Issues in Mental Health Care and Law.

The Evaluation Center will be represented online by Bill Fisher, PhD, Director for Psycho-Social and Forensic Services Research, Department of Psychiatry for the University of Massachusetts School of Medicine, Worcester; and Steve Leff, PhD and Matthew Wise, MPH of HSRI

Contact: Matthew Wise, MPH
The Evaluation Center @ HSRI
2336 Massachusetts Avenue
Cambridge, MA 02140

EVALTEN

Access: E-mail
MAJORDOMO@WORLD.STD.COM

The Evaluation Center @ HSRI has set up an Internet Listserv to provide assistance, information, and contacts regarding experimental design, instrument and survey development, and statistical analysis for mental health systems evaluation. The Network will foster discussion and produce monographs introducing topics such as longitudinal data analysis, cluster analysis, and discriminant and factor analysis to provide stakeholders in mental health systems with sufficient skill to read further on the subject or to use statistical software packages.

This mailing list is part of The Evaluation Center's Topical Evaluation Network on Methodology and Statistics. The Evaluation Center will be represented online by Marcus Lieberman, PhD of the Harvard-Smithsonian Center for Astrophysics, Harvard University; and Steve Leff, PhD and Matthew Wise, MPH of HSRI.

The Evaluation Center @ HSRI is a grant program of the Center for Mental Health Services funded to provide technical assistance related to the evaluation of adult mental health systems change.

Contact: Matthew Wise, MPH
The Evaluation Center @ HSRI
2336 Massachusetts Avenue
Cambridge, MA 02140

IAPSY-L

Access: E-mail
LISTSERV@ALBNYVM1

Interamerican Psychologists List (SIPNET). IAPSY is intended to facilitate and encourage communication and collaboration among psychologists throughout the Americas and the Caribbean, and to aid the Interamerican Society for Psychology/Sociedad Interamericana de Psicologia in its activities. The languages of the list are English, French, Portuguese, and Spanish (the languages of the ISP).

Owner: Bob Pfeiffer
GRAPE@ALBNYVM1

INTERPSYCH

Access: E-mail
MAILBASE@MAILBASE.AC.UK

InterPsych is a nonprofit, voluntary organization, established on Mailbase with the aim of promoting international scholarly collaboration on interdisciplinary research efforts in the field of psychopathology. There are many sublists that are accessed via the main address by indicating, in the body of the e-mail, **Subscribe xxx** where **xxx** is the name of the sublist.

Sublists in this group:

Attachment

This list welcomes discussion on Bowlby-Ainsworth's theory of attachment. From theoretical and philosophical issues to clinical or applied issues. Particular emphasis is given to socio-affective and defensive processes, and unconscious representations.
To join send the message: **join attachment [firstname lastname]** to:
MAILBASE@MAILBASE.AC.UK

Transcultural -Psychology

Discussion of the delivery of mental health services to diverse cultures. Topics may include cultural differences in views on mental disorders, culture-specific syndromes, collaboration between Western and traditional healers, and cultural variance in symptoms.
To join send the message: **join transcultural-psychology [firstname lastname]** to:
MAILBASE@MAILBASE.AC.UK

Psychiatry-Resources

This list is intended for those who wish to cooperate in the compilation of a resource guide to enable clinicians and academics in the areas of psychiatry and abnormal psychology to gain maximum benefit from the facilities available over the Internet.

To join send the message: **join psychiatry-resources [firstname lastname]** to:

MAILBASE@MAILBASE.AC.UK

Psychiatry

Many research findings and viewpoints in psychiatry are controversial, leaving a gulf between those pursuing radically different approaches to mental illness. This forum will act as a bridge between those taking a biomedical approach and those taking a psychodynamic, existential, or behaviourist approach.

To join send the message: **join psychiatry [firstname lastname]** to:
MAILBASE@MAILBASE.AC.UK

Depression

This forum exists for scholarly discussion of issues related to mood disorders in clinical and research settings. Integrative biological-psychological contributions are particularly welcome. Topics include causation, correlates, consequences, comorbidity, treatment/prevention, etc.

To join send the message: **join depression [firstname lastname]** to:
MAILBASE@MAILBASE.AC.UK

Helplessness

Learned Helplessness and Explanatory Style was created to discuss the latest research on animals and humans, biological substratum, depression, anxiety, prevention, CAVE, politics, children, personal control, health, battering, bereavement, PTSD, sex differences, pessimism, work, heritability.

To join send the message: **join helplessness [firstname lastname]** to:
MAILBASE@MAILBASE.AC.UK

Traumatic-Stress

This list promotes the investigation, assessment, and treatment of the immediate and long-term psychosocial, biophysiological, and existential consequences of highly stressful (traumatic) events. Of special interest are efforts to identify a cure of PTSD (Posttraumatic Stress Disorder).

To join send the message: **join traumatic-stress [firstname lastname]** to:

MAILBASE@MAILBASE.AC.UK

Psychiatry-Assessment

This sublist focuses on research and clinical issues related to use of psychological tests (including traditional clinical instruments and normal personality measures) in psychiatry and clinical psychology.
To join send the message: **join psychiatry-assessment [firstname lastname]** to:
MAILBASE@MAILBASE.AC.UK
Contact: All comments and suggestions to:
Ian Pitchford
I.PITCHFORD@SHEFFIELD.AC.UK

PILOTS
Access: For detailed access information see description below

The PILOTS database is an electronic index to the world-wide literature on posttraumatic stress disorder (PTSD) and other mental health consequences of exposure to traumatic events. It is produced by the National Center for PTSD, and is available for searching as a file on the Dartmouth College Library Online System. There is no charge for using the database, and no account or password is required. As of January 1995 there were over 7,000 references (almost all including abstracts) in the database.

For more information on each topic, see the pages indicated by numbers in [brackets] in the PILOTS Database User's Guide. Available from:
Superintendent of Documents
U.S. Government Printing Office
P.O. Box 371954
Pittsburgh, PA 15250-7954
Stock number 051-000-00204-1
Price $19.00 U.S., $23.75 to foreign addresses
Available via FTP from ftp://ftp.dartmouth.edu directory *pub/ptsd*
Logging on by modem [6]—dial (603) 643-6310 for access at 2400 baud or less, or (603) 643-6300 for access at 9600 or 14400 baud
When you see an @ prompt, type **c lib**
At the -: prompt, type **SELECT FILE PILOTS**
Via the Internet [7]—telnet to: lib.dartmouth.edu

At the -: prompt, type **SELECT FILE PILOTS**

For additional information, please contact the National Center at the address below:
Fred Lerner, DLS, Information Scientist
National Center for Post-Traumatic Stress Disorder
VA Medical Center (116D)
White River Junction, VT 05009
Phone: (802) 296-5132
FAX: (802) 296-5135
E-mail PTSD@DARTMOUTH.EDU

SCI.PSYCHOLOGY

Access: Usenet

Psychology issues discussion group.

SCI.PSYCHOLOGY.DIGEST

Access: Usenet

Psychology issues in digest form.

MISCELLANEOUS

COMPMED

Access: E-mail
LISTSERV@WUVMD
LISTSERV@WUVMD.WUSTL.EDU

COMPMED is an unmoderated, open forum for the discussion of comparative medicine, laboratory animals (all species), and related subjects. This list is open to any e-mail user with an interest in laboratory animals and biomedical research. Subject matter may range from, but is not limited to:

- News items
- Meeting announcements
- Research issues
- Information requests
- Veterinary/husbandry topics
- Job notices
- Animal exchange information
- Book reviews

Owner: Ken Boschert
KEN@WUDCM.WUSTL.EDU

HYPBAR-L

Access: E-mail
LISTSERV@TECHNION
LISTSERV@TECHNION.TECHNION.AC.IL

HYPBAR-L is an e-conference to provide an unmoderated environment where issues, questions, comments, ideas, and procedures can be discussed. In a broad sense, this includes virtually anything dealing with medicine in relation to diving and HyperBaric Medicine. The explicit purpose of HYPBAR-L is to provide timely interchange between subscribers, to provide a forum where interesting questions can be addressed within the context of interactive exchange between many individuals, to discuss the evolution and application of HyperBaric and Diving Medicine, to announce professional meetings, calls for papers, and any additional information that would be of interest.

Owner: Derrell Early
BESTUUR@VTVM2
CSM1AL@TECHNION

IVTHERAPY-L

Access: E-mail
LISTSERV@NETCOM.COM

The IVTHERAPY-L list is for communication and mutual support of I.V. therapy nurses and other interested professionals.

NEPHROLOGY

RENALNET
Access: World Wide Web, Gopher
http://ns.gamewood.net//renalnet.html
gopher://gamewood.net/11/renalnet

This site has pointers to nephrology resources, renal biopsy case reviews, and the care of patients with renal disease. Selected biopsy cases include a clinical history, photomicrographs, pathologic diagnosis, and discussion.
Contact: Dr. J Charles Jennette
WILKMAN@MED.UNC.EDU

NEUROLOGY/NEUROSCIENCES

MGH NEUROLOGY
Access: World Wide Web
http://132.183.145.103/

The Gateway to Neurology at Massachusetts General Hospital is a good starting point to travel to a diverse range of neurology and other medical science resources on the Internet, including Harvard's Whole Brain Atlas:
http://www.med.harvard.edu:80/AANLIB.home.html
Contact: John Lester
LESTER@HELIX.MGH.HARVARD.EDU

NEUROSCIENCE INTERNET RESOURCE, V 1.0
Access: World Wide Web, Gopher, FTP
See access below for more information.

This document aims to be a guide to existing, free, Internet-accessible resources helpful to neuroscientists.
Access: An ASCII text version (86K) is available in the Clearinghouse of Subject-Oriented Internet Resource Guides as follows:

- anonymous FTP:
  host: una.hh.lib.umich.edu

    path: */inetdirsstacks*
    file: *neurosci:cormbonario*
- Gopher: via U. Minnesota list of gophers
  menu: North America/USA/Michigan/Clearinghouse.../All Guides/Neurosciences
- WWW
  gopher://una.hh.lib.umich.edu/00/inetdirsstacks/neurosci:cormbonario
  http://http2.sils.umich.edu/Public/nirg/nirg1.html

Contact: Sheryl Cormicle and Steve Bonario
School of Information and Library Studies
University of Michigan
E-mail NIRG@UMICH.EDU

NEUROSCIENCES ON THE INTERNET

Access: World Wide Web
http://ivory.com/~nab/

There are many neuroscience resources to explore on the Internet through World Wide Web browsers and other tools. The first section of this page lists sites that are ideal starting points for this exploration by virtue of their composition and/or numerous links. Subsequent sections list some biological and medical resource sites and World Wide Web sites invaluable for any type of information retrieval.

Contact: Neil A Busis
NAB@TELERAMA.1M.COM

TBI-SPRT

Access: E-mail
LISTSERV@SJUVM
LISTSERV@JUVM.STJOHNS.EDU

Traumatic Brain Injury list exists for the exchange of information by survivors, supporters, and professionals concerned with traumatic brain injury and other neurological impairments which currently lack a forum.

Owner: Len Burns
LBURNS@CATS.UCSC.EDU or
LABYRIS@GORN.ECHO.COM

Neurosurgery

MASSACHUSETTS GENERAL HOSPITAL NEUROSURGERY

Access: World Wide Web
http://neurosurgery.mgh.harvard.edu./fnctnlhp.htm/

Neurosurgery Web server includes information (and several newsletters) covering radiosurgery, aneurysms, arteriovenous malformations, neuroendocrine tumors, spinal and peripheral nerve surgery, functional and stereotactic surgery, pediatric neurosurgery, and neurogenetics.

Contact:
Dr Stephen Tatter
TATTER@HELIX.MGH.HARVARD.EDU
Dr Robert Carter
CARTER@HELIX.MGH.HARVARD.EDU
C. Owen
OWEN@HELIX.MGH.HARVARD.EDU

NEUROSURGERY

Access: E-mail
LISTSERV@GIBBS.OIT.UNC.EDU

A NEUROSURGERY e-mail list is now available to provide a forum for discussion of all aspects of neurosurgery, including clinical, basic science, academic, socioeconomic, and political. The mailing list facilitates communication between individuals interested in these topics.

Contact: David McKalip
MD Division of Neurosurgery
University of North Carolina
Chapel Hill, NC
Phone: (919) 966-1374
DMMCKALI@GIBBS.OIT.UNC.EDU.

Nuclear Medicine

LARGNET NUCLEAR MEDICINE RESOURCES

Access: World Wide Web

http://johns.largnet.uwo.ca/nucmed/index.html

Largnet offers a calendar of meetings, reports from meetings, nuclear medicine programs, and notices of program availability at this site.

NUCMED-REQUEST

Access: E-mail
NUCMED-REQUEST@UWOVAX.UWO.CA

Discussion of Nuclear Medicine and related issues. Of particular concern is the format of digital images.

OBSTETRICS AND GYNECOLOGY

BREAST DISEASES—MULTIMEDIA COURSEWORK

Access: World Wide Web
http://mystic.biomed.mcgill.ca/MedinfHome/MedInf/Breastcourse/html-text/home/BreastHome.html

From McGill University Medical School, a WWW page for teaching third-year medical students breast diseases. Currently includes: anatomy, histology, breast lump management, chemotherapy, and surgical procedures.

MENOPAUS

Access: E-mail
LISTSERV@PSUHMC
LISTSERV@PSUHMC.MARICOPA.EDU

Menopause Discussion List. MENOPAUS is an open list for the discussion of menopause and the sharing of remedies and personal experiences related to menopause. It's open to women of all ages and other interested parties. While the list is meant to be a casual discussion list, people from the medical community are also welcome.

Owner: Judy Bayliss

UMMC-OBSTETRICS AND GYNECOLOGY

Access: World Wide Web

http://www.anes.med.umich.edu/obgyn/index.html

The University of Michigan Medical Center obstetrics and gynecology home page provides information on consultation, comprehensive treatment planning, and a broad range of services for patients with normal- and high-risk pregnancies; gynecologic oncology and urology, prenatal diagnostics, and many other services. Physician queries are welcomed.
Please call M-LINE at (800) 962-3555

Contact: Peggy Phillips
PHILLIPP@UMICH.EDU

WMN-HLTH

Access: E-mail
LISTSERV@UWAVM
LISTSERV@UWAVM.U.WASHINGTON.EDU

CWHR Introduces its Women's Health Electronic News Line. The Center for Women's Health Research is starting an electronic newsletter and discussion group for people who are interested in women's health and can access e-mail on internet or BITNET.

Owner: Shirlee Cooper
SHIRLEE@CARSON.U.WASHINGTON.EDU

ONCOLOGY

ONCOLINK

Access: World Wide Web
http://cancer.med.upenn.edu/

This cancer information server is aimed at physicians. Subject headings include: medical oncology, radiation oncology, pediatric oncology, surgical oncology, medical physics, psychosocial support for oncology patients and families, links to other oncology centers in the world.

Contact: Dr. E. Loren Buhle, Jr.
BUHLE@XRT.UPENN.EDU.

OPHTHALMOLOGY

INTERNET OPHTHALMOLOGY

Access: World Wide Web
http://ubvms.cc.buffalo.edu/~oopraym/ophthal.html

From SUNY at Buffalo Department of Ophthalmology, this resource is for residents and ophthalmologists and related staff. It contains case presentations, summaries of the literature, CME resources, and a catalog of ophthalmology Web sources. Clinical cases and journal reviews placed on this site will also be disseminated through the OPHTHAL listserv list (see below).
Contact: OOPRAYM@UBVMS.CC.BUFFALO.ED

LIVE-EYE

Access: E-mail
LISTSERV@YORKVM1
LISTSERV@VM1.YORKU.CA

Color and Vision Discussion Forum, LIVE-EYE is to be used as a discussion forum. It will not be closely monitored. This is an excellent place to conduct discussions on any topic relevant to color science and/or vision research. LIVE-EYE is an adjunct to the Color and Vision Network (CVNet).
Owner: CVNET@VM1.YORKU.CA

OPHTHAL

Access: E-mail
LISTSERV@UBVM.CC.BUFFALO.EDU

OPHTHAL is a moderated and edited mailing list for Ophthalmology. It concentrates on the practice of clinical ophthalmology. Anonymous clinical case presentations, management decisions, treatment options, and positions available are appropriate for posting.
Contact: Ray Magauran
OOPRAYM@UBVMS.CC.BUFFALO.EDU

OPHTHALMOLOGY DISCUSSION GROUP

Access: E-mail
OOPRAYM@UBVMS.CC.BUFFALO.EDU

This is an ophthalmology professionals' discussion group. Send e-mail requesting to be added to the list distribution.

Contact: DRPEPPER@POSTOFFICE.PTD.NET

SCI.MED.VISION

Access: Usenet

Vision and eyecare issues.

ORTHOPAEDICS

BACKS-L

Access: E-mail
LISTSERV@MOOSE.UVM.EDU

A discussion list concerning research on low back pain and resulting disabilities.

Owner: Elizabeth H. Dow
EDOW@MOOSE.UVM.EDU

OANDP-L

Access: E-mail
LISTSERV@NERVM.NERDC.UFL.EDU

The OANDP-L list is intended for clinical orthotists and prosthetists, researchers, physicians, therapists, and all others with an interest in the science of Orthotics and Prosthetics. For a scope of this list see, e.g., The Journal of Prosthetics and Orthotics and Prosthetics and Orthotics International.

OANDP-L is operated under the patronage of the Orthopaedic and Orthotic and Prosthetic Department at Shands Hospital at the University of Florida. The list will be moderated.

Owner: Paul E. Prusakowski, CO

PRUSAPE.REHAB@SHANDS.UFL.EDU

OTORHINOLARYNGOLOGY

EAR STRUCTURE CT IMAGES
Access: World Wide Web
http://www.sbu.ac.uk/SAS/dirt/EAR_CT.html

These images, from the Central Middlesex Hospital, London, examine the relationship between ear structure and function.

PATHOLOGY

GASTROINTESTINAL AND LIVER PATHOLOGY
Access: World Wide Web
http://www.pds.med.umich.edu/users/greenson/

This page, from the University of Michigan, offers liver and infectious disease pathology along with selected "Cases of the Month."

LARGNET MEDICAL I-WAY
Access: World Wide Web
http://johns.largnet.uwo.ca:80/info/keywords.html

This assortment of case presentations is arranged by anatomic location and includes images. Clicking on an anatomic group shows a case list. Clicking on a pathological group shows cases based on a selection of pathological groups. The cases include case histories, images, clinical diagnoses, and case comments.
Contact: Justin Billinghay
JBILLING@JULIAN.UWO.CA

PATHOLOGY: VIRTUAL LESSONS
Access: World Wide Web
http://virgil.mc.vanderbilt.edu/Virgil_Lessons/Complete_List.html

Located at Vanderbilt University, this multimedia course includes educational reviews of the adrenal gland, ischemic heart disease, tumors, lung infections, etc.

USUHS PATHOLOGY WEB SERVER
Access: World Wide Web
http://wwwpath.usuf2.usuhs.mil

The Uniformed Services University of the Health Sciences Department of Pathology offers continuing medical education units that complement the completion of its on-line educational program.
Contact: Paul Fontelo
FONTELO@USUHSB.USUHS.MIL

SURGICAL PATHOLOGY CASES/IMAGES
Access: World Wide Web
http://www.bgsm.wfu.edu/Surgicals/cases.html

Cases, images, and microscopic diagnoses from Bowman Gray School of Medicine.

PEDIATRICS

THE AMERICAN ACADEMY OF PEDIATRICS
Access: World Wide Web
http://www.aap.org/dogl/dogl.html

World Wide Web page for the American Academy of Pediatrics.

BEHAVIOR
Access: E-mail
LISTSERV@ASUACAD

Behavioral and emotional disorders in children discussion list.
Owners: Samuel A. DiGangi ATSAD@ASUACAD
Robert B. Rutherford Jr. ATRBR@ASUACAD

CSHCN-L

Access: E-mail
LISTSERV@NERVM.BITNET
LISTSERV@NERVM.NERDC.UFL.EDU

An electronic interactive discussion network for individuals with shared interests, both professional and personal, in children with special health care needs. Recent topics of discussion have been managed care, health care reform, accessing services, and exploring needs of families with children with special health care needs. CSHCN-L is a service provided by the Institute for Child Health Policy (ICHP) at the University of Florida through a grant from the USPHS Maternal and Child Health Bureau.

Owner: Donna Hope Wegener, MA
DONNAHOPE_WEGENER@QM.SERVER.UFL.EDU

PCCSG

Access: E-mail
LISTPROC@ITS.MCW.EDU

Moderated clinical research forum in which health care professionals discuss issues relevant to multiinstitutional studies in pediatric intensive care.

Owner: Carl G.M. Weigle, MD

PEDIATRIC ONCOLOGY GROUP PAGE

Access: World Wide Web
http://pog.ufl.edu/

Pediatric Oncology Group, a collaborative research group, is dedicated to the treatment of childhood cancers. Descriptions of eligibility qualifications and specific chemotherapy regimens are offerred. Over 100 member institutions and more than 2,500 patients per year are registered on these research protocols.

PEDIATRIC-PAIN

Access: E-mail
MAILSERV@AC.DAL.CA

This is an international forum for discussion of any topic related to pain in children. Appropriate subjects might include: clinical problems or questions, research problems or proposals, announcements of meetings, book reviews, and political or administrative aspects of children's pain management and prevention.

PEDIHEART

Access: E-mail
HEART@MEDISUN.UCSFRESNO.EDU

A mailing list for discussions about pediatric cardiology. Send e-mail to request being added to the mail distribution.

RADIOLOGY CASES IN PEDIATRIC EMERGENCY MEDICINE

Access: FTP
ftp://ftp.hawaii.edu

This program requires Microsoft Windows 3.1 and a 256-color driver. It contains 20 cases and over 60 radiographic images. Good for medical student teaching, resident teaching, and continuing medical eduation. Download the program file *xr1.zip* via FTP from in the outgoing subdirectory. You may obtain this program (U.S. and Canada only) by mailing two 3.5 inch high density disks to the address below.

Dr. Yamamoto will copy the program onto your disks and mail them back to you. There is no charge for this. You are encouraged to copy the disks and distribute them to others.

Contact: Loren Yamamoto, MD
University of Hawaii
Department Pediatrics,
1313 Punahou Street, #716
Honolulu, HI 96826

PHARMACOLOGY

ANCHODD

Access: E-mail

LISTSERV@CC.UTAS.EDU.AU

A mail list for the exchange of information between drug scientists to share skills and resources and identify potential research partners.

PHARMACOLOGY HOME PAGE

Access: World Wide Web, Gopher
http://farmr4.med.uth.tmc.edu/homepage.html
gopher://farmr4.med.uth.tmc.edu:70

Maintained by the Department of Pharmacology at the University of Texas Houston Medical School. Good collection of educational resources in pharmacology.
Contact: David Loose-Mitchell
DLOOSE@FARMR1.MED.UTH.TMC.EDU

PULMONARY MEDICINE

COMPREHENSIVE LUNG CENTER (CLC)

Access: World Wide Web
http://www.clc.upmc.edu/

The University of Pittsburgh Medical Center has created the Comprehensive Lung Center to be a comprehensive pulmonary diagnostic and treatment resource for both physicians and patients.

NCE-RESP

Access: E-mail
LISTSERV@MCGILL1

Network of Centers of Excellence in Respiratory Health discussion list.
Owner: Whitney Devries
WHITNEY@CHRISTIE.MEAKINS.MCGILL.CA

RC_WORLD

Access: E-mail

LISTSERV@INDYCMS
LISTSERV@INDYCMS.IUPUI.EDU

RC_WORLD list is open to all health professionals who wish to discuss Respiratory Therapy or Respiratory Care issues. Nurses, physicians, and respiratory care practitioners are welcome to discuss health care reform, patient-focused care delievery models, and respiratory care outside the U.S. The list is open to submissions by nonsubscribing health professionals. Replies will normally be sent to all subscribers. Indiana University Medical Center, Department of Respiratory Care, is the institutional host of the list.

Owners:
John A. Hannigan, RRT
JHANNIG@INDYCMS.BITNET
JHANNIG@INDYCMS.IUPUI.EDU
David C. Farr, CRTT
DFARR@INDYCMS.BITNET
DFARR@INDYCMS.IUPUI.EDU

RADIOLOGY

BRIGHAMRAD

Access: World Wide Web
http://www.med.harvard.edu/BWHRad/

Brigham and Women's Hospital house radiology files that describe diagnostic and interventional imaging procedures. They also have continuing medical education courses and a nuclear medicine electronic teaching file.

CHORUS

Access: World Wide Web
http://chorus.rad.mcw.edu/chorus.html

CHORUS—Collaborative Hypertext of Radiology—is a quick reference for physicians and medical students describing diseases, radiological findings, differential diagnosis lists, and anatomy, pathology, and pathophysiology. Documents are indexed by organ system and are connected by hypertext links.

Contact:
Charles E Kahn, Jr, MD
Chu-Peng Felicia Cheong

RADIOLOGY SOCIETY OF NORTH AMERICA (RSNA)

Access: World Wide Web
http://www.rsna.org/

Contains information about research, education and practice resources, membership information, the RSNA annual meeting, and tables of contents from issues of the journal, *Radiology*.

Contact: WEBMASTER@RSNA.ORG

SCI.MED.RADIOL

Access: Usenet

Radiology discussion group.

WEB RADIOLOGY TEACHING FILES LIST

Access: World Wide Web
http://www.xray.hmc.psu.edu/

This site from Penn State maintains links to all radiology teaching files arranged alphabetically by body system or subject.

NURSING/ALLIED HEALTH

AMERICAN JOURNAL OF NURSING COMPANY

Access: World Wide Web
http://www.ajn.org:80/

This site, maintained by the American Journal of Nursing Company, provides on-line access to several journals, including the *American Journal of Nursing*, *Nursing Research*, and *The American Journal of Maternal/Child Nursing*; and a choice of e-mail forums or "chat rooms" for discussion of the information provided by the home page.

Contact: Jack Peterson
JACK.PETERSON@AJN.ORG
John Kelly
JOHN.KELLY@AJN.ORG

DIET

Access: E-mail
LISTSERV@NDYCMSI

Support and discussion of weight loss.

Owner: Roger Campbell
CAMPBELL@UBVM

FALL PREVENTION SUPPORT

Access: FTP
ftp://ftp.csn.org

Tactilitics, Inc., the makers of the RN+ OnCall Bed Monitoring system, has established a Fall Prevention data site on the Internet. This data site is used to support the Fall Prevention Network and to support RN+ OnCall users. The information available includes research abstracts, RN+ product announcements, and Fall Prevention Network support services for practicing nurses and quality assurance persons. This data site is provided as a public service to fall prevention professionals.

HOMEHLTH

Access: E-mail
LISTPROC@ITS.MCW.EDU

HOMEHLTH is an open discussion of management, operations, and technical issues facing home health care management executives. The purpose of this listserv is to site a friendly and open discussion among the senior and midlevel management of home health agencies, hospices, home infusion therapy providers, and suppliers of durable medical equipment, prosthetics, orthotics, and supplies. Participation from the public, private, and academic sectors is welcome.

Owner: Carl G. M. Weigle, MD
PICU-REQUEST@ITS.MCW.EDU

NUTRICION HUMANA WEB (HUMANA NUTRITION HOME PAGE)

Access: World Wide Web
http://www.spin.com.mx/nutrimex/nutrimex.html

From Mexico City, this Web site brings together many human nutrition sources on the Internet. It includes FTP, telnet, WWW, Gopher, on-line newsletters, Usenet, Listservers, Seminars, FAQs, etc. Spanish language, but links are English.

Contact: J. Angel Ledesma S.
Clinical Nutritionist
JLEDESMA@SPIN.COM.MX

NELSON INSTITUTE OF ENVIRONMENTAL MEDICINE

Access: World Wide Web
http://charlotte.med.nyu.edu/HomePage.html

Part of New York University Medical Center, the Nelson Institute is one of the oldest centers for research into the health effects of environmental pollution. This site contains an alphabetical listing of publications from 1989 to 1994.

Contact: D. J. James
DJJAMES@CHARLOTTE.MED.NYU.EDU

NIGHTINGALE

Access: World Wide Web, Gopher
http://nightingale.con.utk.edu:70/0/homepage.html
gopher://nightingale.con.utk.edu:70

A major nursing resource maintained at the University of Tennessee, Knoxville College of Nursing. It contains links to professional nursing communications, colleges and universities, and research information.

NURCENS

Access: E-mail
LISTSERV@UNCVM1

NURCENS is a network discussion group for nurses associated with or interested in nursing centers (nurse-run clinics affiliated with schools of nursing).

NURCENS has been established to enable computer network-based discussions that can enhance and enrich consultations among nurses about nursing centers.

Contact: Forward questions regarding NURCENS to:
P. Allen Gray, Jr., RN, PhD
307 Church Street
Wilmington, NC 28401
Phone: (919) 251-8518
FAX: (919) 395-3863
GRAY@VXC.UNCWIL
GRAY@VXC.UNCWIL.EDU

Owners:
P. Allen Gray
GRAY@VXC.UNCWIL.EDU
Doug Cutler
UNCDWC@UNCVM1

NURSE WWW INFORMATION SERVICE

Access: World Wide Web; Gopher
http://www.csv.warwick.ac.uk:8000/
gopher://nurse.csv.warwick.ac.uk/

Includes links to a wide range of nursing resources on the Internet. A new electronic journal is also being launched from this site, which is maintained at the Department of Nursing Studies, School of Medicine, University of Birmingham, UK.

Contact: Denis Anthony
Phone: ++ 44 121 414 3572
Fax: ++ 44 121 414 4036
ANTHONDM@SUNL.BHAM.AC.UK

OCC-ENV-MED-L

Access: E-mail
MAILSERV@MC.DUKE.EDU

OCCUP-ENV-MED provides a forum for announcements, dissemination of text files, and academic discussion. The forum is designed to allow presentation of clinical vignettes, synopses of new regulatory issues, and reports of interesting items from publications elsewhere (both the medical and the nonmedical journals).

The Association of Occupational & Environmental Clinics represents the first nucleus of members for the list and will use the list for announcements. AOEC members are either:

A. Interested clinics with approved credentials documenting expertise in Occupational and Environmental Medicine.
B. Individuals interested in sharing this topic but who have no requirement to show advanced training or expertise.

Professional affiliations of the Mail list subscribers will include:
- Occupational Physicians and Nurses
- Industrial Hygienists
- Government Public Health Officials
- University Investigators and Regulators in Occupational and Environmental Medicine diseases.

Topics may include:
- Case Presentations, ending with What do I do next?
- Ethical concerns
- Requests for technical expertise, usually free and off-the-cuff.
- Requests for collaborators, either research or business.
- Announcements of hot topics, including regulatory issues, case reports with effect on usual practice, news events.
- Job postings and requests for offers.

Owner: Gary Greenberg, MD
Occ-Env-Med Sysop
GREEN011@ACPUB.DUKE.EDU

PHYSICIAN ASSISTANT WEB PAGE

Access: World Wide Web
http://www.halcyon.com/physasst/

This is the national resource on the net for and about the Physician Assistant profession.

Contact: John Schira, PA-C
JCS@HALCYON.COM

PHNFLASH

Access: E-mail
LISTSERV@TOME.WORLDBANK.ORG

PHNFLASH is an electronic newsletter on key population, health, and nutrition issues, produced by the Population, Health and Nutrition Department in the World Bank. This department is solely responsible for its content.

PHYSIOTHERAPY WWW SERVER

Access: World Wide Web
http://cutl.city.unisa.edu.au/pt/index.html

Maintained at the University of South Australia for the benefit of the international PT (Physiotherapy/Physical Therapy) community, this site aims to be a "one-stop shop" for all PT-related information on the Internet.

Contact: Allan Christie
Centre for University Teaching & Learning
University of South Australia
Phone: (618) 302-2570
FAX: (618) 302-2766

UNIVERSITY OF PENNSYLVANIA POPULATION STUDIES CENTER GOPHER

Access: Gopher
gopher://lexis.pop.upenn.edu:70/1

PSC Data On-Line includes the following information:

AMA (American Medical Association)
CPS (Current Population Survey)
Census Data/Heuser Birth Rate Data
NHANES (National Health and Nutrition Examination Survey)
NLMS (National Longitudinal Mortality Survey)
NMIHS (National Maternal and Infant Health Survey)
NSFH (National Survey of Families and Households)

HEALTH EDUCATION/INFORMATION

BIOETHICS ONLINE SERVICE
Access: Gopher, Telnet
Detailed access instructions below

The Bioethics Online Service is an information resource of the Center for the Study of Bioethics and the Health Information Technology Center (HITC) of the Medical College of Wisconsin (MCW).
The Bioethics Online Service consists of:

A. The Bioethics Database—an update service providing information on current bioethics topics, including news reports, abstracts of pertinent journal articles, legislative actions, and court decisions, with intermittent commentary. The information is searchable by key words.
B. The Bioethics Center and Wisconsin Ethics Committee Network (WECN) News and Announcements section posts news from the Bioethics Center, including speakers, conferences, journal clubs, and other presentations. It also posts news of the Wisconsin Ethics Committee Network and information about its Speakers Bureau. A second feature of this section is a case discussion area.
C. The Bioethics Online E-mail Service allows users to send messages world-wide to those users of the Bioethics Online Service who have e-mail addresses through the Medical College of Wisconsin or have Internet addresses. You must have an Outreach Account or a Post Account through the Medical College of Wisconsin, or have an Internet address to be able to utilize the Bioethics Online E-mail Service.

Using the Bioethics Database gopher:

The Bioethics Database menu has several numbered options. Select an option with the up/down arrow keys and <RETURN>. Note that each menu entry ends with a special symbol. These symbols identify each menu entry as follows:

/ Item is a directory
. Item is a text file
<?> Item is a search index
<CSO> Item is a CSO phone book
<TEL> Item is a telnet session
<) Item is a sound (looks like a speaker)

By noting the symbols at the end of each entry you will know what to expect when selecting a given menu choice. For example, if the menu entry you select ends with a "/" you will see another directory of choices; if it is a "." a text file is presented; etc. (Note: the Bioethics Database does not support <CSO> or <) entries.)

After viewing a text file, you have the option of saving it to a file, printing it, or sending it to someone's mailbox (Note: MIN users without accounts are provided only the mail option). All printing occurs remotely at the ITS (Information Technology Systems) computer room. Please do not print files unless you are a local MCW user. All output is retrieved at the MCW ITS office.

The Bioethics Database is menu-driven and very user friendly. A help screen is always available by typing **?**. Traverse up menu levels with **u** (for "up"). Quit at any time with **q**.

If you have technical questions or problems, please contact the MCW Information Technolgy Systems office. Bioethics Online Service users with E-mail (MCWConnect or MCW Post Accounts) or Internet users may send comments or questions to:

BIOHELP@ITS.MCW.EDU

Otherwise you may send comments or questions to:
Bioethics Online Service
c/o Information Technology Systems
Medical College of Wisconsin
8701 Watertown Plank Road
Milwaukee, WI 53226
Phone: (414) 257-8700

You may also send comments or questions about the content of the service to:
Arthur R. Derse, MD, JD
Bioethics Online Service Director
Center for the Study of Bioethics
Medical College of Wisconsin
8701 Watertown Plank Road
Milwaukee, WI 53226
Phone: (414) 257-8498
ADERSE@ITS.MCW.EDU

Access:
a. by modem and telephone line to MCW:

i. For those with an MCWConnect Account at MCW: dial (800) 699-3282 or (414) 266-5777 at any baud rate. At the prompt (HITC:) type **c outreach** and press <RETURN>. At the menu, select **Internet** and press <RETURN>. At the next menu, select **Gopher** and <RETURN>. Finally, select "Bioethics Online Service" and press <RETURN>.

ii. For those with a Post Account at MCW: dial (414) 266-5777 at any baud rate. At the prompt (HITC:) type **c post** and press <RETURN>, then at the prompt (post) type **bioethics** and press <RETURN>

iii. For those who have neither a Post Account or an MCWConnect Account at MCW:

Obtain an MCWConnect Account from MCW. An MCWConnect Account provides access to the Bioethics Online Service, including a Bioethics Online E-mail account, and access to Internet which includes access to a cornucopia of medical databases, library resources, discussion groups, and electronic mail.

The MCWConnect Account can be reached toll free at (800) 699-3282. It may also be reached by dialing (414) 266-5777.

An MCWConnect Account subscription is $18/year (which includes password, login insructions, user support, and first 2 hours of connect time. On-line connect time is $9/hour.

To get further information about MCWConnect or to apply for an account, contact the Library Systems Office at MCW at (414) 778-4290.

Wisconsin Ethics Committee Network members may also reach the Bioethics Online Service Database and Bulletin Board (minus all the other capabilities including e-mail and Internet access) by dialing (414) 266-5777. At the prompt (HITC:) type **c min** and press <RETURN>, then select the "Bioethics Online Service" option on the menu.

All Wisconsin Ethics Committee Network members are encouraged to take best advantage of the service by obtaining an MCWConnect Account.

b. via the Internet:

i. Using a Unix-based system with a gopher client. If you are accessing the Internet through a Unix-based system and have a Gopher /WWW client, you may access the Bioethics Online Service at:
gopher://post.its.mcw.edu:72

ii. Using Unix-based system utilizing telnet (without a gopher client). If you are accessing the Internet through a Unix-based system but do not have a gopher client, you may access the Bioethics Online Service by typing **telnet://min.lib.mcw.edu** then selecting the "Bioethics Online Service" option on the menu

iii. Using gopher on systems other than Unix. Gopher clients are available from the University of Minnesota for Macintosh, IBM-PC compatible, IBM VM/CMS, and Unix-based systems via anonymous FTP from:
ftp://boombox.micro.umn.edu
Directory *pub/gopher*

Any questions? Send e-mail to:
BIOHELP@POST.ITS.MCW.EDU
Arthur R. Derse, MD, JD
Associate Director for Medical and Legal Affairs
Center for the Study of Bioethics, MCW

BIOMED-L#

Access: E-mail

This is a discussion list concerning the topic of Biomedical Ethics. Since the fields of medicine and medical technology are rapidly changing and are so broad, it is difficult to have clearly delineated rules as to what should and should not be discussed. Possible topics for this list might include: paternalism, fetal cell transplant, the right to die, AIDS, suicide, patient autonomy, abortion, drug legalization, euthanasia, respirator withdrawal, transplants, allocation of scarce resources, and many others too numerous to list here. The discussions may be ethical, philosophical, religious, political, social or even, in some cases, personal. Open discussion, disagreement, and dissent is encouraged. Open flames are most certainly NOT.

Owner: Bill Sklar
86730%LAWRENCE.BITNET@VM1.NODAK.EDU
86730@VM1.NODAK.EDU

CADUCEUS

Access: E-mail
CADUCEUS is not on a Listserver. To subscribe, send a request to:
CADUCEUS@UTMBEACH.BITNET

This is a History of Medicine Collections Forum. CADUCEUS is a moderated discussion group organized for members of the Archivists and Librarians in the History of Health Sciences and other individuals interested in medical history collections. The purpose is to provide a forum for the exchange of information about the administration of special collections in medical history.

Owner: Inci Bowman

HEALTH EDUCATIONAL TECHNOLOGY WEB SERVER
Access: World Wide Web
http://wwwetb.nlm.nih.gov

A Web server on information relevant to educational technology in the health professions is now available. The server is maintained by the Educational Technology Branch (ETB) at the National Library of Medicine. The server features information about Branch research and personnel and provides links to other closely related Web and Gopher servers. ETB runs a Learning Center for Interactive Technology at the NLM in Bethesda, Maryland. Details about the Center and on how to arrange for an appointment to visit us are also provided.

Please contact us if you would like to see something else on this server, including links to other related Web or Gopher servers.

Contact: Alexa McCray
National Library of Medicine
MCCRAY@NLM.NIH.GOV

HEALTHMGMT
Access: E-mail
LISTSERV@CHIMERA.SPH.UMN.EDU

HEALTHMGMT is an unmoderated Internet discussion forum for those interested in the practice, research, and education of management in health care and health service organizations. Discussions on issues pertaining to the management and administration of all health-related organizations, including hospitals, health systems, HMOs, nursing homes, health care networks, etc., and debates about current issues and events in health care and their impact on health care organizations and research are all welcomed. Management practitioners, researchers, and educators interested in health care issues are all encouraged to participate. Enrollment is open to anyone interested in these issues. HEALTHMGMT is also the electronic discussion list for the Health Care Administration Division of the Academy of Management.

HEALTHNET
Access: World Wide Web

http://debra.dgbt.doc.ca/~mike/home.html

HealthNet is a demonstration project undertaken by Industry Canada to help highlight the potential of existing communications technologies that can be applied toward the development of a health care information infrastructure for Canada.

Contact: Health Information Infrastructure (HII) Consulting
C34 Columbus Ave, Suite 1
Ottawa, Ontario
Canada K1K 1R3

HHSCOM-L

Access: E-mail
LISTSERV@NIHLIST

Although open to subscription, the list is primarily for staff within the U.S. Department of Health and Human Services. It focuses on the use of resources available on the Internet, improving HHS use of communication technology, and improving HHS access to information available within and outside of the Department.

Owner: Bob Raymond
OSASPE.SSW.DHHS.GOV
Office of the Assistant Secretary for Planning and Evaluation.
Phone: (202) 690-7316

HIM-L

Access: E-mail
LISTSERV@FIONA.UMSMED.EDU

The purpose of HIM-L is to:

A. Facilitate the transition of medical record practitioners to health information managers.
B. Discuss current legislative, accreditation, and regulatory issues affecting the HIM field.
C. Provide a forum for health information management educators to share educational strategies.
D. Develop joint student projects within and between HIM programs.

E. Provide interaction for HIM students with educators and students from other HIM programs.

F. Provide an opportunity for HIM students to practice using a Listserv.

HYPERMED

Access: E-mail
LISTSERV@UMAB

Biomedical Hypermedia Instructional Design discussion list.
Contact: Kent Hisley
KHISLEY@UMAB

NAT-HLTH

Access: E-mail
LISTSERV@TAMVM1.TAMU.EDU

NAT-HLTH Health Issues of American Native Peoples.

PANET-L

Access: E-mail
LISTSERV@YALEVM
LISTSERV@YALEVM.CIS.YALE.EDU

Medical Education and Health Information discussion list. This discussion list is intended to provide a forum for the sharing of those seeking Health for All in the Year 2000. The Dominant language is English, although some information appears in Spanish. Membership is open to all nationalities and health care disciplines, although emphasis is on Latin America and the field of medicine. The e-conference is a collaborative effort between the Health Manpower Development Office (HSM) of the Pan American Health Organization and the Panamerican Federation of Associations of Medical Schools (PAFAMS).
Owner: Wendy Steele
STEELE@MCS.NLM.NIH.GOV

PBLIST

Access: E-mail
MAILSERV@UTHSCSA.EDU

MAILSERV@UTHSCSA.BITNET

The PBLIST list exists to promote discussion of problem-based learning (PBL) in health sciences education. Topics may include case writing; tutoring and training of tutors; collaboration between departments and institutions; student perspectives on PBL; research and experiences with PBL in various courses and institutional settings; evaluation methods; and the fostering of collegial relationships in support of the goal of this list. The owners hope that interpersonal computing will enhance the use of PBL in health sciences education and bring together those educators and students who wish to share their thoughts on this subject.

Owners/Moderators:
Tom Deahl
DEAHL@THORIN.UTHSCSA.EDU
Bill Hendricson
HENDRICSON@UTHSCSA.EDU

QP-HEALTH
Access: E-mail
MAJORDOMO@QUALITY.ORG

This is a list for the discussion of quality-related issues in health care for health care professionals. It provides a means for multidisciplinary and cross-functional discussions of health care quality issues. Suggested areas for discussion include information systems, ethics, health care regulation, human resources, and quality of care and services.

Contact: Raymond R. Blank
Administrator, QP-Health
RBLANK@HEALTHCARE.ORG

SHS
Access: E-mail
LISTSERV@UTKVM1
LISTSERV@ UTKVM1.UTK.EDU

Student Health Services discussion list. The purpose is to promote the widespread and rapid exchange of information among the medical and administrative staffs of student health services of institutions of higher education.

Owners:
Dr. Jo G. Sweet
SWEET@UTKVX
Bruce Delaney
PA6460@UTKVM1

HEALTH CARE REFORM/ECONOMICS

CLINTON HEALTHCARE SECURITY ACT (HSA)

Access: Gopher
gopher://mchnet.ichp.ufl.edu

A long and detailed analysis of the Clinton Health Care Security Act, prepared by Allan Bergman and Bob Griss of United Cerebral Palsy Association.

This analysis is based on a preliminary draft of the President's health reform proposal dated September 7, 1993 unless otherwise specified. The Consortium for Citizens with Disabilities (CCD) adopted five principles as the basis for a disability perspective on health care reform. These are: (1) nondiscrimination; (2) comprehensiveness; (3) appropriateness; (4) equity; and (5) efficiency.

Available on the MCHNET gopher. Gopher address is:
gopher://mchnet.ichp.ufl.edu
The document is saved as *Analysis/Clinton HlthPlan*

Contact: Allan Bergman or Bob Griss
United Cerebral Palsy
1522 K Street, Suite 1112
Washington, DC 20005
Phone: (202) 842-1266/(800) USA-5UCP

If you have problems connecting with the MCHNET gopher or would like an electronic copy of this document sent to you via the Internet, contact:
JOHN_REISS@QM.SERVER.UFL.EDU

FINAN-HC

Access: E-mail
LISTSERV@WUVMD

Health Care Financial Matters Discussion List. This list is designed to enhance the exchange of information and ideas among members interested in teaching and research in health care finance. Finance is broadly interpreted to include accounting, economics, and insurance. While most discussions will focus on U.S. issues, international concerns are encouraged. Membership applicants should introduce themselves by speaking about their relevant interests and/or experiences.

Owner: Robert Woodward
RSW@WUBIOS.WUSTL.EDU

HEALTHPLAN

Access: E-mail
SFREEDKIN@IGC

White House Health Plan. This Internet mailing list is a conduit through which the White House sends health reform announcements directly to health professionals and others with E-mail addresses.

Owner: Steve Freedken
SFREEDKIN@IGC.APC.ORG

HEALTHRE

Access: E-mail
LISTSERV@UKCC.BITNET
LISTSERV@UKCC.UKY.EDU

Health Care Reform. The purpose of Health Reform (HealthRe) is to share information and opinions, ideas, and inquiries that relate to the topic of health care reform. While this is high in the political life of the U.S. at the present, observations, comments, or opinions on health care reform in other countries are welcome.

Owners:
Eleftheria Maratos-Flier
EMARAT@HARVARDA.HARVARD.EDU
Rick Narad
RNARAD@OAVAX.CSUCHICO.EDU
Bob Moore
STR002@UKCC

HUMAN SERVICES RESEARCH INSTITUTE (HSRI),

Access: Gopher
gopher://gopher.std.com

The Evaluation Center at HSRI has set up 4 Topical Evaluation Networks: National Health Care Reform, Outcomes Evaluation, Legal and Forensic Issues in Mental Health, and Evaluation Methodology and Statistics. The purpose of this program is to provide mental health system stakeholders (consumers, providers, researchers, and families) with the opportunity to communicate directly with each other, and with Evaluation Center Associates about topics of specific interest in adult mental health system change evalution.

Contact:
Human Services Research Institute
The Evaluation Center
2336 Massachusetts Avenue
Cambridge, MA 02140
Phone: (617) 876-0426
FAX: (617) 492-7401
JSH@HSRI.ORG
JSH@MAX.TIAC.NET

LIST.HEALTHPLAN

Access: Gopher, FTP
gopher://sunsite.unc.edu

Users of the Alliance for Progressive Computing (APC) networks, including PeaceNet, EcoNet, HomeoNet, and LaborNet on the Institute for Global Communications (IGC) system, may read any of the past postings in the (c)onference LIST.HEALTHPLAN.

Gopher is menu-based, and you can access past LIST.HEALTHPLAN postings by choosing the following menus. (NOTE: Please read the text of the menus; it is possible the numbers may change from time to time.) Worlds of SunSITE—by Subject/Browse All Sunsite Archives/academic/political-science/*whitehouse-healthcare.archive/*

FTP: ftp://sunsite.unc.edu in the directory *pub/academic/political-science/whitehouse-healthcare.archive*

from here the articles are broken down by year:

drwxr-xr-x 7 health other 512 Dec 7 06:27 1993

You will also see a 1994 directory.
drwxr-xr-x 2 health other 512 Nov 24 15:12 Aug
drwxr-xr-x 2 health other 512 Dec 22 06:55 Dec
drwxr-xr-x 2 health other 1024 Dec 20 17:18 Nov
drwxr-xr-x 2 health other 2048 Dec 20 17:18 Oct
drwxr-xr-x 2 health other 1536 Nov 24 15:25 Sep

MHCARE-L

Access: E-mail
LISTSERV@MIZZOU1
LISTSERV@MIZZOU1.MISSOURI.EDU

Discussion of topics pertaining to Managed Health Care and Continuous Quality Improvement.

Owner: Andrew Balas
MEDINFAB@MIZZOU1

NATIONAL HEALTH SECURITY ACT

Access: Gopher
gopher://calypso.oit.unc.edu/11/sunsite.d/politics.d/health.d

Search the text of the National Health Security Act (FILE) Letter to Tom Foley and George Mitchell, Oct 27th 1993.

- The President's report on health care
- The full text of the Health Security Act
- Address to Joint House of Congress—As Delivered
- The President's speech–Prepared Remarks to Congress
- The Need For Reform
- Executive Summary
- National Health Security Plan—Summary

MEDFINANCE

Access: E-mail
LISTMANAGER@HOOKUP.NET

MEDFINANCE is a mailing list for discussing financial issues relevant to health care in Canada. Examples of topics of discussion in this group include:
- Changes to the health care system
- Fee caps and billing policies
- Private practice costs and investments
- Uninsured services
- Investment frauds and scams targeting doctors
- Other personal finance issues

The list is run by the *Medical Post's Outlook*, Maclean Hunter's financial magazine for Canadian physicians. For those of you who do not receive *Outlook*, we will post to the list selected articles from each issue. In addition, we will solicit policy statements and newsletters from Canadian government health agencies and medical associations to provide our members with a rich information source and help you keep up with changes in the medical financial world.

Although this group is targeted specifically at Canadian issues, physicians from around the world are invited to join, to share their experiences, and to learn from those of others.

Contact:
Charles Jaimet and Don Marston
Medical Post's Outlook
AO878@TORFREE.NET
DMARSTON@HOOKUP.NET

RISK
Access: E-mail
LISTSERV@UTXVM.CC.UTEXAS.EDU

Provided as a means of electronically distributing communications related to issues concerning the general topic of risk management and insurance. Originally created as a discussion group of the American Risk and Insurance Association, but nonmembers may subscribe. Of interest to hospital risk managers.

WHITE HOUSE HEALTH PLAN
Access: Gopher
gopher://gopher inform.umd.edu

The White House health plan.

Directories: *Educational Resources/United States/Government/White House/Press Releases/Health Care*

INFORMATICS/COMPUTERS

AMIA-37

Access: E-mail
LISTSERV@UMAB
LISTSERV@UMAB.UMD.EDU

American Medical Informatics Association discussion list. This list coordinates e-mail for the members of the American Medical Informatics Association's Professional Specialty Group on Emergency Medicine Anesthesiology, and Critical Care (PSG-37). This group focuses on issues pertinent to the application of medical informatics within the patient care continuum represented by these medical specialties.

Owner: Ron Benoit
RBENOIT@COUNT.AB.UMD.EDU

C-HEALTH

Access: E-mail
LISTSERV@IUBVM
LISTSERV@IUBVM.UCS.INDIANA.EDU

The C-Health discussion group is intended to promote sharing of information, experiences, concerns, and advice about computers and health. This list is intended to promote sharing of information, experiences, concerns, and advice about computers and health. Anecdotal evidence, media reports, and some formal studies suggest that computer users are at risk from misuse and overuse of computers. Eyestrain, headache, carpal tunnel syndrome, and other apparently computer-related maladies are increasing. And it would appear that many institutions have been slow to respond with education, training, office and lab design, etc.

Owner: Kimberly Updegrove
KIMU@DAIRP.UPENN.EDU

CBR-MED

Access: E-mail
LISTPROC@CS.UCHICAGO.EDU

The CBR-MED mailing list provides a forum for the discussion of CBR methods in medicine. The list brings together medical practitioners, health informaticians, and CBR researchers in service of two goals:
1. To support the delivery of medical care by fostering the development of CBR software that performs health care-related tasks.
2. To spur the development of CBR methods by focusing the efforts of researchers on the challenges (large databases, knowledge representation problems, etc.) provided by medical and health informatics problems.

Contact:
Jeff Berger
Kurt Fenstermacher
OWNER-CBR-MED@CS.UCHICAGO.EDU

CENTER FOR ADVANCED MEDICAL INFORMATICS AT STANFORD (CAMIS)

Access: Gopher
gopher://camis.stanford.edu/1

The Center for Advanced Medical Informatics at Stanford (CAMIS) is a shared computing resource supporting research activities in biomedical informatics at the Stanford University School of Medicine. Information includes:

Internet-Wide Title Search

This is an index search similar to the Local (CAMIS) Title Search, but for the entire Internet. There is currently no Boolean capability (obviously), nor partial word or phrase searching.

Bio-Medical and Related Gophers

This directory contains pointers to other Gopher sources that include medical schools, medical publications, genetic engineering, computational biology, etc.

CAMIS (Center for Advanced Medical Informatics at Stanford)

This directory contains information such as Technical Report Abstracts, the SMI Publication List, a schedule of colloquia, journal club, seminars, and other documents and resources useful to student and staff of the Section on Medical Informatics (SMI).

Computing Info

This directory contains computing information for the Section on Medical Informatics (SMI) community as well as that of the Knowledge Systems Laboratory (KSL). Additionally, pointers to information outside SMI and KSL are included. These include various index searches of various Frequently Asked Question (FAQ) archives.

COCAMED
Access: E-mail
LISTSERV@UTORONTO

Computers in Canadian Medical Education discussion group.

Owner: Grace Paterson
GRACE.PATERSON@DAL.CA

COLUMBIA PRESBYTERIAN LIBRARY OF MEDICAL LOGIC MODULES (MLM KNOWLEDGE BASE)
Access: FTP
ftp://cucis.cis.columbia.edu
Login **anonymous**
Directory *pub/mlm*

It is also available via gopher, which you can telnet to:
telnet: cuhsla.cpmc.columbia.edu
login: **infoseeker**
choose: *Health Sciences Resources at CPMC*

The medical knowledge base is composed of units called *Medical Logic Modules* (MLMs) written in the Arden Syntax.
The Arden Syntax for MLMs is a language for encoding medical knowledge. Each MLM contains sufficient logic to make a single medical decision. MLMs

have been used to generate clinical alerts, interpretations, diagnoses, screening for clinical research, quality assurance functions, and administrative support.

With an appropriate computer program (known as the *Event Monitor* at CPMC), MLMs run automatically, generating advice where and when it is needed. For example, one MLM warns physicians when a patient develops new or worsening kidney failure.

The Arden Syntax was designed specifically for sharing knowledge. This collection contains MLMs donated by a number of different institutions. Some institutions have supplied only the maintenance and library information from the MLMs for free distribution; the knowledge section is missing. If you want the full versions, contact:

Johanne La Grange
LAGRANG@CPMAIL-AM.CIS.COLUMBIA.EDU

Note that these MLMs have a validation level of testing and no domain specialist has been entered. This means that they are NOT validated for clinical use in their current form. If you use them, you must take responsibility for testing them and making sure they are appropriate for your institution.

Contact: George Hripcsak, MD
HRIPCSA@CUCIS.CIS.COLUMBIA.EDU)

COSTAR

Access: E-mail
COSTAR-CMRS-REQUEST@UNIXG.UBC.CA

Members of the AMIAComp Med Rec Work Group list may be interested in subscribing to a complementary list which focuses on propagating news, questions, answers, and debate relating to the COSTAR (Computer STored Ambulatory Record), which was first developed at the Massachusetts General Hospital for the Harvard Community Health Plan. It is now in the public domain and has been implemented in 500 sites world-wide including a network of 23 Canadian and U.S. Multiple Sclerosis research clinics.

Contact: Donald Studney MD
Department of Medicine
University Hospital
2211 Wesbrook Mall
Vancouver, BC
CANADA V6T 2B5
Phone: (604) 822-7142
FAX: (604) 822-7141

CPRI-L

Access: E-mail
LISTSERV@WWW.KUMC.EDU

Computerized Patient Records Institute discussion list.

Owner: Lee Hancock
LHANCOCK@KUMC.WPO.UKANS.EDU

FAM-MED

Access: E-mail
LISTSERV@GACVAX1
LISTSERV@GAC.EDU

Use of computer technology in the teaching and practice of Family Medicine.

Owner: Paul Kleeburg, MD
PAUL@GACVAX1

FAM-MED MEDICAL REFERENCES

Access: Gopher
gopher://gopher.gac.edu:70/11/Libraries and Reference/Medical References

Fam-Med Medical Gopher useful to Family Physicians interested in information technology.

Contact: Paul Kleeburg
PAUL@GAC.EDU

HEALTH SCIENCES LIBRARIES CONSORTIUM SOFTWARE DATABASE

Access: World Wide Web
http://www.einet.net/hytelnet/FUL050.html

The Health Sciences Libraries Consortium Computer Based Learning Software Database. It houses listings of IBM-PC compatible and Macintosh programs used in health sciences education.

Contact: Jerilyn Garofalo
GAROFALO@SHRSYS.HSLC.ORG

HL-7

Access: E-mail
HL-7-REQUEST@VIRGINIA.EDU

Health Level Seven (HL-7) is an electronic conference designed to foster communication concerning technical, operational, and business issues involved in the use of the HL-7 interface protocol. It is also intended as a forum for the HL-7 Working Group members who are participating in the specification of the interface protocol. Health Level Seven is an application protocol for electronic data exchange in health care environments.

This HL-7 Conference is not an official part of the HL-7 Working Group and Executive Committee. Official inquiries concerning HL-7 should be sent directly to:

Health Level Seven
P.O. Box 66111
Chicago, IL 60666-9998
FAX: (708) 616-9099

In accordance with current CREN regulations, commercial activity (such as the selling of software) will be prohibited. Subscription to this conference is open to anyone interested.

All requests to be added to or deleted from this e-conference, problems, questions, etc., should be sent to:

HL-7-REQUEST@VIRGINIA.EDU

Owner: David John Marotta
Medical Center Computing, Stacey Hall
Univ of Virginia
Box 512 Med Cntr
Charlottesville, VA 22908
Phone (work): (804) 982-3718
Message: (804) 924-5261
FAX: (804) 296-7209
DJM5G@VIRGINIA.EDU
DJM5G@VIRGINIA

HL7 IMPORT/EXPORT (HL7IMEX)

Access: World Wide Web, FTP
http://dumccss.mc.duke.edu/ftp/standards.html

ftp://dumcc ss.mc.duke.edu
Login **anonymous**

Health Level 7 (HL7)—HL7 is a protocol for formatting, transmitting, and receiving data in a health care environment. This site provides a collection of functions that can be reused in programs to support HL7 Standard version 2.1. Functions support building, encoding, and retrieval operation with HL7 messages. HL7 is written in C and has implemented at CPMC for AIX (RS/6000). It has also been compiled and run at other sites (DOS, VMS, Sun OS, etc.)

Access:
ftp> cd pub/hl7/hl7imex
ftp> binary
ftp> get hl7imex.2.tar.Z or hl7imex2.zip
> uncompress ...
> tar -xvf ...
> make

The file *./doc/hl7imex.doc* explains how to use the library. There is an example in *./demo*.

Contact: If you have any problems building or using HL7ImEx, suggestions, complaints, etc., contact:
SIDELIR@CUCIS.CIS.COLUMBIA.EDU

If you are unable to access the Internet you can obtain a copy of the software on a DOS formatted diskette by contacting:
Mark D. McDougall
Executive Director
Health Level Seven
900 Victors Way, Suite 122
Ann Arbor, MI 48108 USA
Phone: (313) 665-0007
Fax: (313) 665-0300

HQ-L
Access: E-mail
LISTSERV@PSUHMC

HQ-L (HealthQuest Products Discussion List) is a list to discuss software created and supported by HealthQuest. Examples include, but are not limited to: Clinical Data Editor (CDE), Clinipac, Medical Records Enhancement/Abstract, Patient Accounting (Medipac and/or Medipac III), Patient Appointments, Patient Management (PM), and Trendstar.

Owner: Jeff Schlader
JSCHLADE@PSUHMC

HSPNET-L

Access: E-mail
LISTSERV@ALBNYDH2

Hospital computer network discussion group HSPNET-L provides consultation, a monthly digest, and a database of hospital networks. It emphasizes restoration and extension of consulting for rural hospitals by connection to major medical centers. All aspects (hardware, software, staff training, confidentiality of patient data, etc.) will be covered. Particular attention will be paid to existing networks both in the U.S. and abroad.

HSPNET-D is the Digest of HSPNET-L

All requests to be added to or deleted from this e-conference, problems, questions, etc., should be sent to the owner.

Owner: Donald F. Parsons M.D.
DFP10@ALBNYVM1

INHEALTH

Access: E-mail
LISTSERV@RPIECS
LISTSERV@VM.ECS.RPI.EDU
For more information send this message to:
BITNET: COMSERVE@RPIECS or
Internet: COMSERVE@VM.ECS.RPI.EDU
Help Topics Hotlines

International Health Communication discussion list. InHealth is a Comserve hotline.

Owner: Comserve Editorial Staff
SUPPORT@RPITSVM

LISTER HILL NATIONAL CENTER FOR BIOMEDICAL COMMUNICATIONS (LHNCBC)

Access: World Wide Web
http://www.nlm.nih.gov/lhc.dir/lhncbc.html

The Lister Hill National Center for Biomedical Communications (LHNCBC) was established in 1968 as a research and development arm of the National Library of Medicine, part of the U.S. National Institutes of Health in Bethesda, MD.

The LHNCBC is divided into five branches:

- Communications Engineering Branch (CEB)
- Computer Science Branch (CSB)
- Educational Technology Branch (ETB)
- Information Technology Branch (ITB)
- AudioVisual Program Development Branch (APDB)

One of the activities of the LHNCBC is development of the Unified Medical Language System (UMLS) Project. Other research activity at the LHNCBC includes work on scientific visualization and virtual reality, medical expert systems, natural language processing, computer-aided instruction, machine learning, and biomedical applications of high-speed communication techniques.

Contact: Daniel Masys, MD, Director

MCMASTER UNIVERSITY EVIDENCE BASED MEDICINE PROJECT

Access: World Wide Web
http://hiru.mcmaster.ca/

The Health Information Research Unit at McMaster University offers a number of evidence-based medicine projects online, including links to the international Cochrane Collaboration, the Ontario Health Care Evaluation Network, the Evidence Based Medicine Working Group, and the Clinical Informatics Network.

Contact: Robert S.A. Hayward, MD, MPH, FRCPC
HAYWARDR@MCMASTER.CA

MEDICAL INFORMATICS LAB

Access: World Wide Web
http://ipvaimed9.unipv.it/

The Medical Informatics Laboratory of the Department of Computers and Systems Science (University of Pavia, Italy) proudly announces the birth of its WWW server. The server will be devoted to the documentation of the research activities of the laboratory. The Laboratory is involved in several high-level projects and international collaborations that are mainly focused on the medical applications of Artificial Intelligence and various aspects of Medical Informatics in general.

Contact:
WEBMASTER@IPVAIMED.UNIPV.IT

MEDINF-L

Access: E-mail
LISTSERV@DEARN

Biomedical Informatics Discussion Group. E-conference for people working in medical data processing/medical informatics. All other requests to be added to or deleted from this e-conference, problems, questions, etc., should be sent to:
PL_REI%DHVMHH1.BITNET@CUNYVM.CUNY.EDU
Owner: Dr. Claus O. Koehler, Prof.
DOK205@DHDDKFZ1

MEDITECH-L

Access: E-mail
MAJORDOMO@NIC.III.NET

MEDITECH-L is a mailing list and discussion group for any users or potential users of Meditech's Medical Information Software. The purpose of MEDITECH-L is to bring together Hospital Information System Professionals and End Users for discussion relating to Meditech's software.

- To share information.

- To facilitate communication of standard bugs.
- To maintain contact between MUSE meetings.
- To give those hospitals which cannot attend MUSE meetings at the international level access to other Meditech users outside of their region.
- To give hospitals contemplating purchasing Meditech Software a forum to ask questions.
- To share user-created solutions such as NPR Report Writer Reports and Global Data Search Reports.
- To provide a forum for hospitals searching for Information Systems professionals with Meditech software experience.

Subscribers to this list may be IS professionals, physicians, residents, medical students, nurses, hospital administrators, or anyone who uses any of the wide range of Meditech Modules for various hospital computing tasks. Subscribers are encouraged to send messages of interest to:
MEDITECH-L@NIC.III.NET

MEDITECH-L is currently an unmoderated list. Any postings are automatically accepted.

SCI.MED.TELEMEDICINE
Access: Usenet

Medical Networking—Hospital Networks discussion group.

TELEMED_PRIMARY_CARE
Access: E-mail
LISTSERV@CC.UCH.GR

Telemedicine in primary health care, networking primary health care units in order to exchange data, statistics made easy through telemed networks, Hippocrates System, prospects of telemedicine, telemedicine via the Internet.
Contact: Dim. Papadimitriadis
PAPADIMI@HIPPOCRATE.MED.UCH.GR
TELEMED_PRIMARY_CARE-OWNERS@CC.UCH.GR
Under the auspices of The Medical School of Crete.
Professor Mihalis Fioretos
Assistant Prof. Christos Lionis

TELEMEDICINE GLOSSARY

Access: World Wide Web
http://kellogg.cs.hscsyr.edu/Telemedicine/glossary.html

Explanations of telemedicine terms plus pointers to examples at the Health Science Center at Syracuse, New York.

TELEMEDICINE IN NEW YORK STATE PART 1, V1.01

Access: E-mail
LISTSERV@ALBNYDH2.BITNET

The latest version can be obtained by sending the command:
get hspnet-l nystelem asc

This is an Electronic Publication: NYS Summary Readers are encouraged to send the author descriptions of missing or new network projects. They will be included in updated versions or in Part 2 of this paper.

Existing major New York State medical networks are described. The public and private nonmedical networks are also described since it is believed that some of these networks can economically include medical applications in their traffic flow. The growing deployment of ISDN provides a less expensive wide-bandwidth connection medium for the large number of places where fiber optics cannot yet be justified. It is already in use for several video-consulting projects in the state. The largest medical network is in western New York, and it is supported by a consortium of Buffalo hospitals. The larger VA hospitals are now engaged in a pilot study involving transmitting the complete medical record (including the x-rays).

The New York City Health Department has contracted to exchange medical records and patient management data between the larger city hospitals. Obstacles to the growth of telemedicine are discussed.

Access: To retrieve the complete paper, send the message, **GET NYS SUMMARY** to: LISTSERV@ALBNYDH2.BITNET

Contact: Address for correspondence:
Wadsworth Center, Room C273
NY State Department of Health
ESP, Box 509
Albany, NY 12201-0509

DFP10@ALBNYDH2.BITNET
Phone: (518) 474-7047
FAX: (518) 474-7992

TELEMEDICINE WEB PAGE

Access: World Wide Web
http:// naftalab.bus.utexas.edu/~mary/tmpage.html

Telemedicine projects, research, unpublished studies, etc.

Contact: Mary Moore
Doctoral Fellow
U. Texas/Austin Library
MMOORE@FIAT.GSLIS.UTEXAS.EDU

UCSF CLINICAL DATABASE RESEARCH PROGRAM

Access: World Wide Web
http://cdrp.ucsf.edu/cdrp_whatis.html

This Clinical Database Research Program points investigators to clinical data in machine-readable form. Included are computerized data from UCSF, inpatient admissions, medical records, laboratory information, and outpatient laboratory and demographic information.

Contact: Thomas B.Newman, MD, MPH, Director
NEWMAN@CDRP.UCSF.EDU

GRANTS AND CAREERS

GRANTS

D-PERIO

Access: World Wide Web, Gopher
See the description below for access information.

World Wide Web:
http://medoc.gdb.org/best/fed-fund.htm

Informational conversation of NIDR grantees or potential grantees on the general topic of periodontal disease. Federally-Funded Research in the U.S. is a series of databases that provide information about research funded by the federal government. These databases contain the names and addresses of principal investigators, grant titles, abstracts, and keywords associated with grants funded by the National Institutes of Health (NIH), National Science Foundation, the U.S. Department of Agriculture (USDA), the Small Business Innovation Research Program (SBIR), and the Advanced Technology Program (ATP).

Gopher:
gopher://gopher.mountain.net:70/11/grants

A wide variety of public and private grant funding information. This section contains information on grants and funding collected from sites all over the U.S.

Remember that links to other sites can be down at any time, making some files temporarily unavailable. If you find that a file is consistently unavailable, report it to the address below. If you have or know of information that you would like added here, send electronic mail to:
GOPHER@GOPHERHOST.CC.UTEXAS.EDU

The information in this section is maintained by the providers listed below. Providers are responsible for the accuracy and timeliness of their data. Report problems or suggestions to the appropriate provider. Most providers have "About files" that describe their offerings. Read these files for detailed information; brief descriptions are below.

Deadlines: By Agency

Deadlines and brief descriptions for funding programs run by over 275 organizations. Maintained by the University of Kentucky.

Deadlines: By Month

Deadlines and brief descriptions for funding programs, organized by month of deadline. Maintained by the University of Kentucky.

Fedix

Searchable databases on research and educational programs, contracts, equipment grants, and more from the DOE, FAA, NASA, the Office of Naval Research, the Air Force Office of Scientific Research, and other government agencies. Maintained and updated daily by the Federal Information Exchange. Report problems and suggestions to:

GOPHER@FEDIX.FIE.COM

Federal Domestic Assistance Catalog

A catalog of information on assistance programs of the federal government, published by the U.S. Government Printing Office and updated about every 6 months. This copy is stored at the University of Tennessee, Knoxville. Report problems and suggestions to the Printing Office at (202) 783-3238.

Co-Owners:
Dennis Mangan
UFD@NIHCU
Thomas Murphy
TGL@NIHCUNIHLIST

THE ROBERT WOOD JOHNSON FOUNDATION

Access: Gopher
gopher://gopher.rwjf.org:4500

The Robert Wood Johnson Foundation Gopher is designed to be a convenient information resource for people seeking grants and general information about the healthcare sector. It contains general information such as how to apply for grants, the names of officers and staff, a descriptive overview of the Foundation, and contact information. In addition, it contains complete listings of current RWJF calls for proposals and open grants. The full-texts and excerpts of many of the Foundation's publications, including ADVANCES, the Foundation's quarterly newsletter, the annual report, recent news releases, and information derived from selected grants and programs are also available.

The Gopher also includes information about Health Tracking, a new Foundation program examining and reporting on the US healthcare system, and direct links and information about other Gophers of RWJF programs and projects.

Contact:
Ann Seawright, Communications Assistant
The Robert Wood Johnson Foundation
PO Box 2316
Princeton, NJ 08543-2316
AS@RWJF.ORG

NIH

Access: Gopher
gopher://bongo.cc.utexas.edu/11/ut-info/department/grants

Contains the NIH Guide to Grants and Contracts, listings of NIH research interests, data on NIH grantees, and other information for researchers. Maintained by the National Institutes of Health. Report problems and suggestions to:
GOPHER@GOPHER.NIH.GOV

NSF

Contains a searchable index to NSF award abstracts and publications, a database of forms for submitting proposals electronically, and much more. Maintained by the National Science Foundation. Report problems and suggestions to:
STIS@NSF.GOV

Other: Funding Programs—Private and Government

A searchable list and brief descriptions of the funding programs offered by over 300 organizations. Maintained by the University of Wisconsin-Madison. Report problems and suggestions to:
GOPH_ADM@MSD.MEDSCH.WISC.EDU

Other: Funding Programs—Private and Government

A searchable, menu-driven database of information on state and federal grants, economic data, tax information, and more. Maintained by the Texas Comptroller of Public Accounts. Report problems and suggestions while logged on to the system.

Other: Funding and Research Database

A searchable database of over 13,000 funding programs from over 3,000 agencies compiled from various sources. Maintained and updated daily by the University of Tennessee, Knoxville. Off-campus access to some information is prohibited.

Other: The Foundation Center

An international network of over 180 libraries that distribute information about organizations giving grants. At UT Austin, the Hogg Foundation for Mental Health (512-471-5041) is a member of this network. This list is maintained by the University of California, San Francisco. Report problems and suggestions to:

JOED@ITSA.UCSF.EDU

U.S. Department of Education

Announcements (only some of which are related to grants) from the Office of Educational Research and Improvement (OERI) of the U.S. Department of Education. OERI posts this information to a LISTSERV mailing list:
ERL-L@VM.TCS.TULANE.EDU

These announcements are collected and stored by the University of Wisconsin-Milwaukee. Report problems and suggestions to OERI at: JBENTON@INET.ED.GOV

Funding Bulletins from American Psychological Association

Announcements of funding sources for research and training in psychology, posted to a LISTSERV mailing list: APASD-L@VTVM2.CC.VT.EDU

These announcements are collected and stored by the University of Wisconsin-Milwaukee. Report problems and suggestions to the APA at: APASDDES@GWUVM

Templates

Contains templates from various sources for submitting grant proposals and performing other tasks.

Grants and Contracts NIH guide

The information found in this directory has been taken from the electronic form of the NIH Guide to Grants and Contracts available via anonymous FTP from: CU.NIH.GOV

Each edition of the NIH Guide begins with an index, and may contain one or more of the following:

- notices
- notices of availability (RFPs/RFAs)
- ongoing program announcements (PAs)
- errata

All of the above information has been indexed and is searchable. The logical "and" and "or" operators can be used to do multiple keyword searches.
The six folders listed under this directory are described below:
About the NIH Guide—this file.
Search NIH Guide (most recent 6 weeks)—the last six issues of the Guide can be searched here.
Search NIH Guide (Jan 1992 to present)—searches done here include all Guides back to January 1992.

NIH Guide—flat text files—each NIH Guide dating back to January 1992 is listed as a directory (by date).

Request for Applications (RFAs)—full text—contains flat text files for each RFA that is available in a full text form (dating back to January 1992). Note: these files can be very long.

Program Announcements—full text—contains flat text files for each Program Announcement that is available in a full text form (dating back to January 1992). These, too, can be very long.

Questions concerning a specific notice, RFA, RFP, or PA should be directed to the contact person listed in that announcement.

General questions concerning the NIH Guide should be directed to the NIH Institutional Affairs Office at (301) 496-5366.

Questions regarding gopher should be sent to:
GOPHER@GOPHER.NIH.GOV

GRANTS & CONTRACTS BULLETIN BOARD

Access: E-mail, Telnet, Gopher
See the description of services below for access information

The purpose of NIH GRANT LINE is to make program and policy information for the Public Health Service (PHS) agencies rapidly available to the biomedical research community. Most of the research opportunity information available on this bulletin board is derived from the weekly publication NIH Guide for Grants and Contracts consisting of Notices, RFAs, RFPs (announcements of availability), Numbered Program Announcements, and statements of PHS policy. The electronic version known as *E-Guide* is available for electronic transmission each week, sometimes a day or two in advance of the nominal Friday publication date. The material consists predominantly of statements about the research interests of the PHS Agencies, Institutes, and National Centers that have funds to support research in the extramural community.

A monthly listing of new NIH Awards is available. Also available is an order form to obtain NIH publications from DRG's Office of Grants Inquiries. The information found on the NIH Grant Line is grouped into three main sections:

1. Short News Flashes that appear without any prompting shortly after the user has logged on.

2. Bulletins that are for reading.
3. Files that are intended mainly for downloading.

There are menus and simple English commands, but all the user has to type is the first letter of the commands displayed. Since most of the current as well as archived files are located in the section of the bulletin board called FILES, type **F** in order to be able to access any of the files which are arranged into directories. To get an overview of the kinds of information available, type **D** for Directory. Remember that you can mail files (a download option) to your Internet address.

Also included is electronic access to NIH guide for grants and contracts. There are two principal methods of accessing the NIH Guide electronically.

1. Via electronic networks to institutional hubs.
2. By accessing NIH GRANT LINE, an electronic bulletin board

Institutional Hubs
The first method is to have someone in your research setting volunteer to receive the NIH Guide, Indices, and Directories automatically via electronic networks each time they are updated, then redistribute them locally to biomedical researchers. These participants are the institutional hubs. The preferred and most efficient method of distribution is for each hub to disseminate the material by existing systems or by methods of their own choosing. To express your interest in serving as the focal point for your organization and to receive a letter of invitation, send an e-mail message in which the responsible person is named to Dr. Claudia Blair:

BITNET: Q2C@NIHCU
Internet: Q2C@CU.NIH.GOV

NIH GRANT LINE
The other method, which requires active intervention to access the same documents each week, is to get access to the NIH GRANT LINE. Directions for this electronic-like bulletin board system are given below. One feature on NIH GRANT LINE is that users have an option of downloading selected documents through a modem, or the rapid transmission of files via BITNET or Internet to their BITNET or Internet address. If the connection to the electronic bulletin board is through a modem, files will download to a PC file. The user can also speed up the process of accessing files in an interactive session by directing mail as indicated below.

To access NIH GRANT LINE:

1. Configure your terminal emulator as: 1200 or 2400 baud, even parity, 7 data bits, 1 stop bit, Half Duplex.
2. Using the procedure specified in the communication software, call (301) 402-2221. When you get a response indicating that you have been connected, type **,GEN1** (the comma is mandatory) and press <RETURN>; you will be prompted by the NIH system for INITIALS?. Type **BB5** and press <RETURN>. You will then be prompted for ACCOUNT?. Type **CCS2** and press <RETURN>.

Messages and a menu will be displayed that allows the user to read Bulletins or download Files. It should not take too long to become familiar with the contents of the bulletin board and the commands to go back and forth from one section to another. On the NIH Grant Line, back issues of the NIH Guide are found in different directories:

GUIDE90 has issues going back to July 6, 1990.
GUIDE91 has all of the issues in 1991.
GUIDE92 has all of the issues in 1992.
GUIDE93 has all issues to date in 1993.

Although the access is through a modem, transmission of the files selected are much faster through the selection of network transmission.

After selecting a file to be downloaded, choose option 2. 2 — Transmitted to a NUnet, BITNET, or Internet userid and then respond with your e-mail address.

Telnet: At the Open prompt, type **,GEN1** (must include comma)
INITIALS? **BB5**
ACCOUNT? **CCS2**

This will get the user into the DRGLINE Bulletin Board (also known as NIH GRANT LINE at NIH).

WYLBUR.CU.NIH.GOV or
128.231.64.82 NIH-GUIDE

NIH Grants and Contracts Distribution List

NIHGDE-LNIH Guide Primary Distribution—NIH Guide University of Washington distribution list. This List controls the PRIMARY DISTRIBUTION of the electronic form of the NIH Guide for Grants & Contracts from the NIH to institutions participating in this program. As the program is currently defined, each institution on this list will receive one copy of each publication sent and is in turn responsible for redistributing or making available the publication for others at that institution by whatever means the institution deems appropriate.

The BITNET address of this list is:

NIHGDE-L@JHUVM

The Internet address of this list is:
NIHGDE-L@JHUVM.HCF.JHU.EDU

This list has no formal peers, however some institutional representatives on this list are LOCAL List Server lists. These lists may have different list header options than this list and are not managed by the NIH.

Contact: Ms. Becky Duvall
Phone: (301) 496-5366
Institutional Liason Office
Q2C@NIHCU
National Institutes of Health
Building 31, Room 5B31
9000 Rockville Pike
Bethesda, MD 20892

Owner: John Paul Elrod
JPE@JHUVM

CAREERS

ACADEMIC PHYSICIAN AND SCIENTIST

Access: Gopher
gopher://aps.acad-phy-sci.com

Academic Physician and Scientist, a colloborative publication of Academic Physician and Scientist and the Association of American Medical Colleges (AAMC), has a new gopher server which lists open academic medical teaching positions for the 126 U.S. medical schools and their affiliated institutions. The service is free of charge. Openings are listed categorically by specialty and state.

Contact:
To subscribe or advertise a position, please contact our office.
Phone: (916) 939-4242
FAX: (916) 939-4249
INFO@ACAD-PHY-SCI.COM

FSDNURSE

Access: E-mail
LISTSERV@UNCVM1

Federal Service Doctoral Nurses List. FSDNURSE is a network discussion group for Federal Service Nurses with Doctoral Degrees. It serves doctoral-prepared active duty and reserve nurses in the Army, Navy, Air Force, as well as doctoral-prepared nurses in the Red Cross, Veterans Administration, and U.S. Public Health Service.

FSDNURSE has been established to enable network-based discussions that can enhance and enrich consultations among Federal Service Nurses.

Contact: Forward questions regarding FSNURSE to:
P. Allen Gray, Jr., RN, PhD
307 Church Street
Wilmington, NC 28401
Phone: (919) 251-8518
FAX: (919) 395-3863

Owners:
P. Allen Gray
GRAY@VXC.UNCWIL.EDU
Doug Cutler
UNCDWC@UNCVM1

FSG ONLINE CAREER SERVICES

Access: World Wide Web
http://www.gate.net/biotech-jobs/

Searchable lists of job candidates and employment opportunities in the field of medical and biotechnology.

GRADNRSE

Access: E-mail
LISTSERV@KENTVM
LISTSERV@KENTVM.KENT.EDU

The GradNrse is a discussion for practicing nurses. It is moderated and originates at Kent State University, Kent, Ohio. It is intended to provide practicing nurses world-wide a place to give and get information about practice situations from their colleagues.

Owner: Linda Q. Thede, RN, MSN
LTHEDE@KENTVM

MED-TECH

Access: E-mail
LISTSERV@FERRIS.BITNET
LISTSERV@VM1.FERRIS.EDU

There are over 800 other educational institutions offering Med-Tech degrees. This base of interest, plus all the people working in the profession at various hospitals and health care providers, makes for a great opportunity to share with each other relevant information, experiences, questions, and anything of interest to those in this field or planning to join it.

Owner: Robert Lathrop
Ferris State University
Big Rapids, Michigan 49307
G563@MUSIC.FERRIS.EDU

MEDSEARCH AMERICA

Access: Gopher, World Wide Web
gopher://gopher.medsearch.com:9001
http://www.medsearch.com

MSA is a complete Medical Recruitment Resource offering job seekers a free resume database, health care job listings, on-line health care career articles, career resources, and more. The medical or health care job seekers pay nothing for the service and find us to be increasingly valuable for employment in their area of expertise.

Contact:
MedSearch America, Inc.
Phone: (206) 827-4676
FAX: (206) 889-5927
OFFICE@MEDSEARCH.COM

GENERAL/REFERENCE

1990 CENSUS
Access: FTP
ftp://info.umd.edu
Login **anonymous**
Password **guest**
Directory */info/Government/US/Census-90*

1990 Census information, arranged state by state. Commands and file names are case-sensitive; be sure to capitalize as above.

At the next asterisk, type **ls** or **dir** to get a list of the contents. To get the file you want, type **get filename,** where **filename** is the name of the file. Type **quit** to quit. The contents of INFO are also available for reading online if you telnet to: telnet://info.umd.edu and follow the directions.

AHL
Access: E-mail
LISTSERV@GWUVM

American Health Line News Service.

ARL DIRECTORY OF ELECTRONIC JOURNALS, NEWSLETTERS AND ACADEMIC DISCUSSION LISTS
Access: Gopher
gopher://arl.cni.org

Maintained by the Association of Research Libraries, this is a comprehensive list of electronic journals, newsletters, and academic discussion groups (not just biomedical). Announcements of new e-journals are posted to the following list:
NewJour-L@e-math.ams.org
Contact: Ann Okerson
Association of Research Libraries
ANN@CNI.ORG

CLINALRT
Access: E-mail

LISTSERV@UMAB.BITNET

There is a Listserv at umab.bitnet called CLINALRT that exists to distribute the Clinical Alerts. They are not issued frequently.

Owner: Steve Foote
Health Sciences Center Library
Emory University
Atlanta, GA 30322
LIBSF@EMORYU1.CC.EMORY.EDU
Phone: (404) 727-0289

DOCTOR-PATIENT

Access: E-mail
LISTSERV@CC.UCH.GR

Doctor-patient relationship, the most important factors that play a crucial role in the doctor-patient communication, teaching methods in undergraduate/postgraduate medical education. Created by the Department of Social & Family Medicine of the Medical School, University of Crete, Greece.

Contact: Dim. Papadimitriadis
PAPADIMI@HIPPOCRATES.MED.UCH.GR
DOCTOR-PATIENT-OWNERS@CC.UCH.GR
   Under the auspices of The Medical School of Crete.
   Prof. Mihalis Fioretos
   Assistant Prof. Christos Lionis

GFULMED

Access: E-mail
LISTSERV@NDSUVM1

This is for discussion of the Grateful Med software package issued by NIH.

GLOBAL NETWORK NAVIGATOR (MEDICAL TABLE OF CONTENTS)

Access: World Wide Web
http://nearnet.gnn.com/wic/med.toc.html

WWW links to a variety of internet health resources on the World Wide Web. An excellent starting point for exploring the Medical Internet on your own.

HEALTH-L

Access: E-mail
LISTSERV@IRLEARN

Contact: Jill Foster
International Discussion on Health Research
JILL.FOSTER@NEWCASTLE.AC.UK

HEALTH AND CLINICAL INFORMATION (BIOETHICS ONLINE SERVICE)

Access: Gopher
gopher://post.its.mcw.edu:70/11/.health

The main menu takes the user via Internet to gophers and other information servers in a variety of locations around the U.S. These gophers contain primarily health and clinical information but contain other types of information as well.

Contact:
Information Technology Systems (ITS) at 414-257-8700
MCW-INFO@ITS.MCW.EDU

HEALTH SCIENCE RESOURCES ON THE INTERNET

Access: FTP
ftp://ftp2.cc.ukans.edu
/pub/hmatrix as the file *medlst04.zip* (The *04* is the date of the release and will change with updates.)

Also available online on many Gophers and World Wide Web sites.
Compiled by Lee Hancock, The University of Kansas Medical Center, this is a comprehensive index of health science resources available on the Internet/BITNET/Usenet. The list includes Listserv groups, Usenet groups, Freenets, Data Archives, and health science-oriented databases.

HMATRIX-L

Access: E-mail

LISTSERV@WWW.KUMC.EDU

A discussion of on-line health science resources. Of primary interest, but not limited to, are resources available on the Internet. Discussions include where to find information, sounds, images, and software of interest to the health professional and interested layperson. Interested not only in what is available where, but also the quality of resource.

Owner: Lee Hancock
LHANCOCK@KUMC.WPO.UKANS.EDU

THE HOSPITAL WEB

Access: World Wide Web
http://dem0nmac.mgh.harvard.edu/hospitalweb.html

A small but growing list of hospitals on the Web. This list is being compiled with the hope that more hospitals will take advantage of the amazing potential of the World Wide Web. The goal is to provide a simple and globally accessible way for patients, medical researchers, and physicians to get information on any hospital in the world.

IRAMED

Access: E-mail
LISTSERV@JERUSALEM1.DATASRV.CO.IL

This group is for general medical discussions/questions.

JMEDCLUB

Access: E-mail
LISTSERV@ BROWNVM
LISTSERV@BROWNVM.BROWN.EDU

Medical journal discussion club.

MEDNEWS—HEALTH INFOCOM NEWSLETTER

Access: E-mail
LISTSERV@ASUACAD

This newsletter contains health-oriented news articles from around the globe. The HEALTH INFOCOM NEWSLETTER is published once a week. The newsletter is usually quite large, so to facilitate network movement, it is broken up into multiple sections. These are always clearly marked.

MEDICAL ILLUSTRATORS' HOME PAGE

Access: World Wide Web
http://siesta.packet.net/med_illustrator/Welcome.html

The Medical Illustrators' Home Page serves as the Internet hub for medical illustration and related services. Publishers, advertisers, medical schools, doctors, and net surfers from around the globe are all welcome to visit.

MEDICAL MEETING PLACE

Access: World Wide Web
http://www.packet.net/medical/Welcome.html

This site provides the medical community a quick and easy way to register for their next medical meeting or symposium.

Contact: Don Epperson
E-mail MEDICAL@PACKET.NET

MEDLARS: NATIONAL LIBRARY OF MEDICINE DATABASES

Access: For on-line access information, e-mail to the MEDLARS Management Section:
MMS@NLM.NIH.GOV

You will be issued a user identification and password in order to access MEDLINE as well as the other 24 databases maintained by the National Library of Medicine.

MEDLINE

Access: See description

MEDLINE is one of over 20 databases available from the National Library of Medicine.

MEDLINE is accessible via the Internet. An account is required for billing purposes. The user is issued a user identification and password. For more information, send e-mail to:
REF@NLM.NIH.GOV

There is an algorithm for pricing. Since it is paid for by taxes, the prices are modest and have just DECREASED to about $17.00/hr. You can also get information about a software package available for $30 called GRATEFUL MED which allows untrained database searchers and health professionals a menu-driven means of performing searches on many of their databases. In addition, an enhancement to the original program called LOANSOME DOC allows you to order copies of articles that you wish to read from participating medical libraries. It's available for both IBM-compatibles and Mac computers. For information about GRATEFUL MED/LOANSOME DOC, e-mail to:
GMHELP@GMEDSERV.NLM.NIH.GOV

Once you get your user identification/password (which is free) you can search databases directly by telneting to:
MEDLARS.NLM.NIH.GOV

Those institutions which make MEDLINE or other databases available for their students/faculty/clientele pay royalty fees and contractually can allow only members of that institution to search FREE.

NATIONAL LIBRARY OF MEDICINE PUBLICATIONS

Access: Gopher; World Wide Web
gopher://gopher.nlm.nih.gov

National Library of Medicine publications.

ONLINE JOURNAL OF CURRENT CLINICAL TRIALS

Access: World Wide Web, Gopher
Gopher://gopher.psi.com:2347/7?clinical

Searchable database of current clinical trials.

PHYSICIANS' GENRX

Access: Telnet
telnet://genrx.icsi.net

Login **genrx**
Password **genrx**
Select an emulation (usually vt100), then login to the GenRx application as guest

ICS is currently offering Physicians' GenRx Online. Physicians' GenRx is a complete drug reference. Locate drugs by generic name, brand name, or categories. Physicians' GenRx was developed for the PC, Unix, and VMS platform. Yearly subscriptions are available for $99.00 a year.

Contact:
Internet Connect Services, Inc.
Victoria, Texas
Phone: (512) 572-9987

PHYSICIAN REFERRAL ONLINE

Access: World Wide Web, E-mail
http://www.medsearch.com/pro

Physician Referral Online (tm), a subsidiary of MedSearch America, Inc., allows patients to search for physicians in their desired location by specialty, procedures, rates, insurance accepted, foreign languages, board certification, and more. After finding your listing, they will even be able to send you e-mail inquiries on the spot.

This service provides Physicians with a way to grow their practices and hospitals to introduce physicians to the public. To enroll, send e-mail to:
PHYSICIANFORM@MEDSEARCH.COM

Physicians who fill out this form and are verified will receive 6 free months of on-line referral with no further cost or obligation.

Contact: Larry Bouchard
MedSearch America, Inc.
15254 NE 95th Street
Redmond, WA 98052
Phone: (206) 883-7252
OFFICE@MEDSEARCH.COM

RESIDENTS

Access: E-mail
LISTSERV@UTMB.EDU

The RESIDENTS mailing list was formed to provide a forum for medical residents of all specialties to discuss issues related to life as a resident. Residency is universally regarded to be stressful. This group of residents can be supportive of each other during this difficult period by networking on Internet.

Contact: Matt Beckwith,
MATTHEW.BECKWITH@UTMB.EDU

SCI.MED

Access: Usenet

Discussion of medicine and its related products and regulations.

SYNAPSE PROJECT

Access: World Wide Web
http://synapse.uah.ualberta.ca/synapse/00000000.htm

Synapse Publishing gives demonstrations of "Care Maps," Clinical Rating Scales, Clinical Trials, Continuing Medical Education, and Consensus and Guideline Information. Links are provided to Medline citations and abstracts, and more.

Contact: Dr. Andrew Penn
Division of Neurology
University of Alberta
SYNAPSE.INFO@UALBERTA.CA

THE VIRTUAL HOSPITAL

Access: World Wide Web
http://indy.radiology.uiowa.edu/virtualhospital.html

The Virtual Hospital (VH) is a continuously updated medical multimedia database stored on computers and accessed through high-speed networks 24 hours a day. The VH will provide invaluable patient care support and distance learning to practicing physicians.

The VH information may be used to answer patient care questions, thus putting the latest medical information at physicians' fingertips. This same information may be used for Continuing Medical Education (CME), delivering CME to physicians' offices and homes at a convenient time and location. The VH is built on preexisting computer and communication standards and uses the World Wide Web software technology to store, organize, and distribute our multimedia text-books (MMTBs) contained within it. We define a MMTB to be a program that patterns its user interface after a printed textbook. Our MMTBs incorporate functions such as free text searching, the ability to play video and audio clips, and to display an unlimited number of high-resolution images.

Contact:
LIBRARIAN@INDY.RADIOLOGY.UIOWA.EDU

THE WWW VIRTUAL LIBRARY—MEDICINE (BIOSCIENCES)

Access: World Wide Web
http://golgi.harvard.edu/biopages/medicine.htm

A comprehensive listing and links to World Wide Web resources for Biology and Medicine.

YAHOO HEALTH MENU

Access: World Wide Web
http://www.yahoo.com/Health/

A fairly comprehensive list of subject-oriented links to on-line health and medical Internet sites.

Contact:
ADMIN@YAHOO.COM

YALE BIOMEDICAL GOPHER

Access: World Wide Web; Gopher
gopher://Yaleinfo.yale.edu

The Yale biomedical gopher is an effort by the Yale Medical Center to organize biomedical information on the Internet. It is part of YaleInfo, the Yale University gopher. The Yale biomedical gopher has organized Internet biomedical information by specific diseases and biomedical disciplines.

Contact:
GOPHMED@GOPHER.CIS.YALE.EDU

ONLINE MEDICAL LIBRARIES

The following are on-line card catalogs which you may browse. Titles may be ordered through interlibrary loan from your local library. Many of these libraries offer other services such as links to databases and article search for a fee.

ALBERT EINSTEIN COLLEGE OF MEDICINE

Interface: LIS
Access: Telnet
telnet://lis.aecom.yu.edu

At the first screen that says ALT-H PRESENTS A SUMMARY of SPE-CIAL KEYS, press <RETURN> for logo, and a second <RETURN> for the options menu to search OPAC.

To exit: Press the telnet escape key

ARCHIE R. DYKES LIBRARY OF THE HEALTH SCIENCES

Access: Telnet
telnet://kumclib.mc.ukans.edu or telnet://169.147.155.200
2400 baud modems should dial: (913) 588-1040
9600 baud modems should dial: (913) 588-5008

Press <RETURN> two or three times until the address prompt appears. Then type **kumclib**. This will connect you directly to the catalog.

To exit: Select **Disconnect** from the main OPAC menu.

ARIZONA HEALTH SCIENCES CENTER

Interface: OPAC=LS/2000
Access: Telnet
telnet://cat.medlib.arizona.edu or telnet://128.196.106.13
When connected press <RETURN>
At TERMINAL: VT100/T/ press <RETURN>
To exit: type **/exit**

AUDIE L. MURPHY MEMORIAL VETERANS' ADMINISTRATION HOSPITAL

Access: Telnet

telnet://panam2.panam.edu or telnet://129.113.1.3

At the main menu press **3** for Other Library Catalogs.
Press **10** for UTHealth Science Center, San Antonio.
When screen says ENTER LIS type **LIS**.
This brings up the main menu for the University of Texas Health Science Center—San Antonio BLIS.
Select **1** from the BLIS menu
Select **0** from the Library Catalogs menu
Select **3** from the Change Locations menu
To exit: Press <RETURN> twice, then type **QUIT**

CASE WESTERN RESERVE UNIVERSITY SCHOOL OF MEDICINE

Interface: GEAC
Access: Telnet
telent://eagle.lit.cwru.edu

CHSL is holdings code for the Health Center Library and Allen Memorial Medical Library.
When connected, type **library** (must be lower case)
To exit, type **X**

COLORADO HEALTH SCIENCES LIBRARIES

Access: Telnet
telnet://pac.carl.org or telnet://192.54.81.128
Choose terminal type from list (#5=vt100)
Press <RETURN> twice
Choose **#1** Library Catalogs Libraries
Choose **#25** Colorado Health Sciences
To exit type **S** to stop or switch databases, **//EXIT** to end session

Includes the following collections: Association of Operating Room Nurses, C.U. Health Sciences Center, Denver Medical Library, Saint Joseph Hospital, Swedish Medical Center.

COLUMBIA UNIVERSITY COLLEGE OF PHYSICIANS AND SURGEONS

Interface: NOTIS
Access: Telnet
telnet://columbianet.cc.columbia.edu
Select **3** Clio Plus: Library Catalogs
Select **CLIO** Columbia Library
To exit type **Q** to quit

Part of the large Columbia University catalog, CLIO. You can search using MeSH.

CORNELL UNIVERSITY

Interface: NOTIS
Access: Telnet
telnet://cornell.cit.cornell.edu
TN3270 emulation is required
At LOGON screen, press <RETURN>
At CP READ screen, type **Library** and press <RETURN>
To exit type **STOP**

DALHOUSIE UNIVERSITY W.K. KELLOGG HEALTH SCIENCES LIBRARY

Interface: GEAC
Access: Telnet
telnet://novanet.nstn.ns.ca
If asked "What System?" type **NOVANET**
To exit type **END**
Subject searching, option 3, refers to NLM MeSH and to LC subject headings

This library is a member of a consortium currently serving eight academic institutions. The name of the system is NOVANET. On logging in you are looking at the composite holdings. Items prefaced with the code DALWKK or DALPHARM (acy) are local holdings. Not all member collections contain medical or health material. Currently the member institutions are: Dalhousie University Libraries, Technical University of Nova Scotia, St. Mary's University, Mt. St. Vincent University, University College of Cape Breton, University of King's College, Nova Scotia College of Art & Design, Atlantic School of Theology.

DANISH NATURAL AND MEDICAL SCIENCE LIBRARY

DNLB and COSMOS Online catalog and ordering system
Interface: Common Command Language
Access: Telnet
telnet://129.142.160.101
Username: **COSMOS**
   At the CCL: prompt type **DIA ENG** for English
   CCL: **STOP** to end the session and logout
   CCL: **INFO** for screens of general information on the system
   CCL: **HELP** or **?** for windows of screen-specific help
   CCL: **DO** or **!** for a window of possible commands to type
   CCL: **WHY** for a window of the last 16 commands entered
   CCL: **DIA DAN** to change the dialog language to Danish
   CCL: **CCL** to return to this screen

DARTMOUTH UNIVERSITY DARTMOUTH MEDICAL SCHOOL

Interface: Common Command Language
Access: Telnet
telnet://lib.dartmouth.edu
   1. Type your terminal type
   2. Type the command **SELECT FILE [name]**, e.g.,
SELECT FILE CATALOG
SELECT FILE PILOTS
SELECT FILE CORK
To exit type **BYE**

EMORY UNIVERSITY HEALTH SCIENCES CENTER

Access: Telnet
telnet://emuvm1.cc.emory.edu

   The Emory University Health Sciences Center library is included in Emory's on-line catalog, as choice 3 (Health-Sciences Center Library). Please note that this needs tn3270 terminal emulation and that once connected, the logging in and logging out can be difficult.

Press <RETURN> at the first screen

When "CP READ" appears, type **DIAL VTAM**

When VTAM screen appears, type **LIB**

When CICS screen appears, Press <ESC> and then **1**

To exit:

1. **e** to end
2. **4** to logoff
3. type **CSSF** and Press <RETURN>
4. at the point, do whatever necessary to break the connection (usually <F4>)

This system also contains two databases of interest: the *PILOTS* file, an index of literature on posttraumatic stress, and Project *CORK* file, which indexes materials on alcohol and substance abuse.

GEORGETOWN UNIVERSITY MEDICAL CENTER

Interface: LIS

Access: Telnet

telnet://gumedlib2.georgetown.edu

At the login prompt, Type **MEDLIB**

Password **DAHLGREN**

Type **NETGUEST**

Press <RETURN> several times

Select option **1**

To exit press <RETURN> on the menu

Type **Q**

HAHNEMANN UNIVERSITY

Interface: LIS

Access: Telnet

telnet://hal.hahnemann.edu

Login: **HAN**

To exit press <ESC>

HARVARD UNIVERSITY COUNTWAY LIBRARY OF MEDICINE

Interface: NOTIS

Access: Telnet

telnet://hollis.harvard.edu or telnet://128.103.60.31
At Welcome screen, press <RETURN>
Type **HOLLIS** at next screen
Select **HU** for Union Catalog
To exit type **Exit**

The Countway Library of Medicine serves Harvard's Schools of Medicine, Public Health, and Dentistry. The catalog lists books from 1960 to present and journals received from 1981 to 1992 while continuing to add older holdings. Dissertations are also cataloged on HOLLIS.

Author, Title, and Subject searches can be limited to Countway's collection. For author or title, follow your entry with **//fa=md**. For example: **au Harrison p//fa=md** will limit the search of author Harrison to Countway's library.

Subject searches should be conducted with ME and a medical subject heading; that will automatically limit results to Countway library.

HEALTH SCIENCES LIBRARIES CONSORTIUM, INC. (HSLC HEALTHNET)

Interface: SAL
Access: Telnet
telnet://shrsys.hslc.org or telnet://192.100.94.3
To exit type **EX**

The Shared Automated Library System, an on-line catalog of six health sciences institutions, contains the holdings of eight health sciences libraries including:

- College of Physicians of Philadelphia
- Hershey Medical Center/Pennsylvania State University
- George T. Harrell Library
- Medical College of Pennsylvania
- Eastern Pennsylvania Psychiatric Institute Library
- Florence A. Moore Library of Medicine, Philadelphia
- College of Osteopathic Medicine, O.L. Snyder Memorial Library
- Philadelphia College of Pharmacy and Science
- Joseph W. England Library
- Temple University
- Dental/Allied Health/Pharmacy Library,
- Health Sciences Center Library.

INDIANA UNIVERSITY LIBRARIES

Interface:
Access: Telnet
telnet://uis.ucs.indiana.edu
Type **GUEST** <RETURN> at the user id prompt
To exit type **STOP** then **F** to exit

IU contains records for more than 2 million items held by the Indiana University Libraries statewide. IO does not yet contain records for all items owned by the IU Libraries. While many regional campus libraries' entire collections are listed in IO, only one-third of the Bloomington Libraries' holdings are listed. It is possible to search by MeSH (**sm=** subject-medical)

MCMASTER UNIVERSITY—MORRIS

Interface: NOTIS
Access: Telnet
telnet://mcmvm1.cis.mcmaster.ca
Once connected, press **9** on your numeric keypad
Move the cursor to MORRIS and press **S** and then <RETURN>
To exit type **STOP** and then F12 (the <CLEAR> key and F12—this varies depending on local systems.)
Use **sm=** to search for medical subjects. Use LIBDATA to check the circulation status of items (type **=n** at the prompt to toggle between MORRIS and LIBDATA)

MEDICAL COLLEGE OF WISCONSIN MEDICAL INFORMATION NETWORK

Interface: INNOPAC
Access: Telnet
telnet://lis.lib.mcw.edu
Type: **LIBRARY**
To exit type **Q** to quit from main menu

NATIONAL LIBRARY OF MEDICINE LOCATOR

Access: Telnet
telnet://locator.nlm.nih.gov or telnet://130.14.12.1
Login **locator**

The National Library of Medicine has extended its Internet reference services to cover inquiries concerning the history of medicine. Questions concerning only that subject can be sent to:

HMDREF@NLM.NIH.GOV

This address supplements the main NLM reference address. For more general queries:

REF@NLM.NIH.GOV

For assistance with Locator, contact the NLM Reference Section. The NLM toll-free telephone number is (800) 272-4787. The Reference Section may also be contacted through Internet at:

REF@NLM.NIH.GOV

The National Library of Medicine (NLM) is the world's largest biomedical library, with a collection of over 4.9 million items. NLM is a national resource for all U.S. health sciences libraries and fills over ¼ million interlibrary loan requests each year for these libraries. The Library is open to the public, but its collection is designed primarily for health professionals.

The Library collects materials comprehensively in all major areas of the health sciences. Housed within the Library is one of the world's finest medical history collections of pre-1914 and rare medical texts, manuscripts, and incunabula. Most materials are in areas which are closed to the public (closed stacks), and may be requested for use in the appropriate Reading Room. Individuals may not borrow materials from the Library.

Contact: Joyce Backus
Systems Librarian
Public Services Division
U.S. National Library of Medicine
JOYCE_BACKUS@OCCSHOST.NLM.NIH.GOV

NATIONAL MEDICAL LIBRARY—HEBREW UNIVERSITY OF JERUSALEM

Access: Telnet
telnet://aleph.biu.ac.ll
Username: ALEPH
From Main ALEPH menu, type **LB/MLB** (LB is the command to select a library, MLB is the code for the National Medical Library)
Select terminal type. 2=vt100 (Latin only, i.e., no Hebrew fonts)
To exit: **STOP**

Available through the Israeli InterUniversity Computerized Catalog System (ALEPH). We are the National Medical Library, Hebrew University of Jerusalem—Hadassah Medical Organization, Jerusalem, Israel. The library is searchable in Hebrew and other soft fonts using VT320 or VT420 terminal emulation. Use terminal type 17, 18, or 19.

NEW YORK UNIVERSITY MEDICAL, DENTAL AND ENVIRONMENTAL MEDICINE LIBRARIES (MEDCAT)

Access: Telnet
telnet://mclib0.nyu.edu or telnet://128.122.205.70
When connected, type **LIBRARY**
To exit type **D** to disconnect

NORTHEASTERN OHIO UNIVERSITIES COLLEGE OF MEDICINE

Access: Telnet
telnet://scotty.neoucom.edu or telnet://140.220.1.2
Type **neocat** (must be lowercase)
For vt100, just press <RETURN> at prompt
To exit type **QUIT** (this cannot be abbreviated) and follow the menus out

The sequence of menus for getting into the catalog is obvious and user friendly; the catalog is not. The user is greeted with a "?" prompt. Responding with **?** <RETURN> will get the first of several help screens. The basic commands needed are **r** (for retrieve) followed by a word from the catalog (Boolean searching is available) and **t** (for type) to look at retrieved records in the sets. Also contains holdings of 17 affiliated hospitals.

ST. BONIFACE GENERAL HOSPITAL LIBRARIES

Interface: PALS
Access: Telnet
telnet://umopac.umanitoba.ca
At the UML=: prompt, type **BE**
To exit type **$$Soff**

The catalog also includes the collections of the University of Manitoba Libraries and University of Winnipeg Library. The catalog provides access to the collections of three institutions so users should note the on-line prompt to determine which institution they are searching.

If you are using the system for the first time, type **HELP**
If you wish to search both libraries in the system, type **HELP SY**

STANFORD UNIVERSITY LANE MEDICAL LIBRARY

Interface: Common Command Language
Access: Telnet
telnet://elf1.stanford.edu
At "Account ?" type **socrates**
At "OK to proceed?" type **YES**
At "terminal?" type **VT100**
To exit type **END**

The catalog includes the holdings of all the Stanford libraries. After creating a set with the **FIND** command, type **LIMIT LOCATION LANE** to limit your results to Lane Medical Library. There is extensive on-line help.

STATE UNIVERSITY OF NEW YORK AT BUFFALO HEALTH SCIENCES LIBRARY

Interface: NOTIS
Access: Telnet
telnet://bison.cc.buffalo.edu or telnet://128.205.2.22
At the "ATTACHED TO PORT..." message, press <RETURN>
Enter terminal type, such as **vt100**. At the UB logo, press <RETURN>
At the Database Selection Menu, type **BAT** (BAT is the only choice for remote users.)
To exit type **STOP**

The Health Sciences Library materials in BISON include all books, journal titles, audiovisuals and the History of Medicine collection. Besides the Health Sciences Library, BISON includes materials from all other University at Buffalo libraries: Science and Engineering Library, Chemistry/Math Library, ArcPress Lecture and Planning Library, Poetry and Rare Books Collection, Lockwood Memorial Library (social sciences, humanities, business, and government documents), the Law Library, and the Undergraduate Library.

THE NATIONAL INSTITUTES OF HEALTH

Access: Telnet
telnet://library.nih.gov

After the connect message, press <ESC>
To exit type **D** to disconnect from the main menu

THOMAS JEFFERSON UNIVERSITY SCOTT MEMORIAL LIBRARY (THOMCAT)

Interface: LIS
Access: Telnet
telnet://jeflin.tju.edu
vt100 emulation required
At USERNAME prompt type **JEFFLINE**
Choose **1** Library Services
To exit type **E** to exit at Main Menu

UMDNJ UNIVERSITY LIBRARIES HEALTH INFORMATION NETWORK

Interface: LIS
Access: Telnet
telnet://library.umdnj.edu
VT-100 emulation is recommended
At the USERNAME prompt, type **LIBRARY**
You will be prompted to type your last name
At the SELECTION prompt (after entering your name) set the <CAPS LOCK> on.
At the SELECTION prompt on the main menu, type **OC** for the Online Catalog
To exit, go to the main menu and type **QU** at the prompt

UNIVERSITY OF CALIFORNIA—MELVYL

Interface: Common Command Language
Access: Telnet
telnet://melvyl.ucop.edu
Type your terminal type and press <RETURN>
At the Welcome screen type **START TEN** (for the last 10 years), **START CAT** (for the full catalog), **START PE** (for journal holdings)
To exit type **STOP**

Includes the collections of all UC libraries. It is possible to limit to just UC San Francisco, all UC medical libraries, or all UC medical libraries—excluding UCSF. The **MAIL** command will send your search results to you via e-mail.

UNIVERSITY OF COLORADO HEALTH SCIENCES CENTER

Access: Telnet
telnet://pac.carl.org or telnet://192.54.81.128
Choose terminal type from list (**5**=vt100)
Press <RETURN> twice
Choose **#1** Library Catalogs
Choose **#9** U of C Health Sciences Center
To exit type **S** to stop or switch databases,
//EXIT to end session

UNIVERSITY OF HAWAII MEDICAL LIBRARY

Interface: Carl Systems
Access: Telnet
telnet://starmaster.uhcc.hawaii.edu
At the Enter Class prompt, type **LIB**
Select your terminal type (select **5**)
In state Libraries and Databases select **1** Hawaii Medical Library Catalog
To exit type **//EXIT**

UNIVERSITY OF MARYLAND HEALTH SCIENCES LIBRARY

Interface: OPAC=LS/2000 <OP011>
Access: Telnet
telnet://annex.ab.umd.edu or 134.192.1.3
Press <RETURN>
Select **hsl4800**
Press <RETURN>
Select **1** for on-line catalog
At terminal prompt, type **VT100** (upper case)
To exit, press the telnet escape key

UNIVERSITY OF MICHIGAN TAUBMANN MEDICAL LIBRARY

Interface: NOTIS
Access: Telnet
telnet://cts.merit.edu

At "which host?" type **MIRLYN**
Type your terminal type, press <RETURN> at welcome screen, type **MCAT**
Use **sm=** to search for medical subjects
To exit type **STOP**

Part of the University of Michigan Libraries catalog.

UNIVERSITY OF NEBRASKA AT LINCOLN MEDICAL CENTER—MCGOOGAN LIBRARY OF MEDICINE

Interface: LIS
Access: Telnet
telnet://library.unmc.edu
Press <RETURN> at Welcome message
To exit press <RETURN> at Main Menu

UNIVERSITY OF PENNSYLVANIA—FRANKLIN

Interface: NOTIS
Access: Telnet
telnet://library.upenn.edu
Press <RETURN> to wake up the system
Type **VT100** <RETURN> when prompted for a terminal type
Press <RETURN> for list of valid terminal types
Press <RETURN> again
Select **FCAT** from the menu
To exit use the telnet escape key or **Y**

The Biomedical Library catalog is part of the larger University of Pennsylvania catalog. It is possible to search by medical subject (MeSH) sm=ou.

UNIVERSITY OF PITTSBURGH—PITTCAT

Interface: NOTIS.
Access: Telnet
telnet://mvs2.cis.pitt.edu
Select **1** Libraries
Press <RETURN>
Select **PITT**
To exit type **QUIT from PITTCAT screen X**

FALK LIBRARY OF THE HEALTH SCIENCES WESTERN PSYCHI-ATRIC INSTITUTE and CLINIC. Part of the larger University of Pittsburgh catalog. Allows searching by medical subject (MeSH) **sm=**

UNIVERSITY OF TENNESSEE, MEMPHIS HEALTH SCIENCE LIBRARY

Interface: LIS
Access: Telnet
telnet://132.192.1.1
vt100 emulation required
At the Username prompt, type **HARVEY** and press <RETURN>
To exit press <RETURN> at the main library menu

UNIVERSITY OF TEXAS HEALTH SCIENCE CENTER—SAN ANTONIO

Interface: LIS
Access: Telnet
telnet://panam2.panam.edu or telnet://129.113.1.3

This connects to the University of Texas-Pan American.
At the Username prompt, type **PACKEY**
At the main menu press **3** for Other Library Catalogs.
Press **10** for UTHealth Science Center—San Antonio
When screen shows "ENTER LIS" type **LIS**. This brings up the main menu for the University of Texas Health Science Center—San Antonio BLIS
Select **1** from the BLIS menu
To exit press <RETURN> twice, then type **QUIT**

UNIVERSITY OF TEXAS HEALTH CENTER AT TYLER

Interface: LIS
Access: Telnet
telnet://panam2.panam.edu or telnet://129.113.1.3

This connects to University of Texas-Pan American.
At the Username prompt, type **PACKEY**
At the main menu press **3** for Other Library Catalogs
Press **10** for UTHealth Science Center—San Antonio

When screen shows "ENTER LIS" type **LIS.** This brings up the main menu for the University of Texas Health Science Center—San Antonio, BLIS

Select **1** from the BLIS menu

Select **0** from the Library Catalogs menu

Select **2** from the Change Locations menu

To exit press <RETURN> twice, then type **QUIT**

UNIVERSITY OF TEXAS MEDICAL BRANCH AT GALVESTON MOODY MEDICAL LIBRARY AUTOMATED CATALOG

Access: Telnet

telnet://ibm.gal.utexas.edu

Type **0** for vt100

Type **3** at the enter code prompt

Press <RETURN> as the function code

To exit press the telnet escape key

UNIVERSITY OF TEXAS SOUTHWESTERN MEDICAL CENTER LIBRARY

Interface: SIRSI

Access: Telnet

telent://library.swmed.utexas.edu or telent://129.112.7.1

Login **medcat**

Password **LIBRARY**

Press <RETURN> on the next menu

If the main menu looks wrong, Press <CTRL> and O

To exit press the <ESC> key

UNIVERSITY OF TORONTO SCIENCE & MEDICINE LIBRARY

Interface: DRA

Access: Telnet

telnet://vax.library.utoronto.ca

Username: UTLink

Choose DRA System

To exit type **STOP** and then select #8 **Logoff**

UNIVERSITY OF UTAH ECCLES HEALTH SCIENCES LIBRARY

Interface: LS/2000

Access: Telnet

telnet://eccles.med.utah.edu or telnet://128.110.78.1
At the Username prompt, type **GUEST**
At the Kermit prompt, press <RETURN>
At the Select Destination prompt, type **CAT96** and press <RETURN>
At the TERMINAL: VT100/ prompt, press <RETURN>
To exit press the telnet escape key

UNIVERSITY OF VERMONT LIBRARIES DANA MEDICAL LIBRARY

Interface: NOTIS
Access: Telnet
telnet://uvmvm.umv.edu
Use TAB to move to the COMMAND field
Type **LUIS** <RETURN>
When "DIALED TO DOSLIBR" appears, press <RETURN>
To exit press the telnet escape key

The Medical Library catalog is part of the larger University of Vermont catalog. It is possible to search by medical subject (MeSH) using **sm=**

UNIVERSITY OF WALES COLLEGE OF MEDICINE

Access: Telnet
telnet://sun.nsf.ac.uk or telnet://128.86.8.7
At the login prompt, type **JANET**
At the hostname prompt, type **UK.AC.UWCM.LIBRARY**
Type **LOGIN OPAC**
Select **1** for vt100
To exit select **L** from the main menu

UNIVERSITY OF WESTERN ONTARIO ALLYN AND BETTY TAYLOR LIBRARY

Interface: GEAC
Access: Telnet
telnet://library.uwo.ca or telnet://129.100.2.18
Terminal type **VT100**
Press <RETURN> (SEND)
To exit press <Ctrl> and **D** simultaneously to disconnect from the system

The Allyn and Betty Taylor Library at the University of Western Ontario serves ALL the sciences, which include all the physical/natural sciences (Chemistry, Geology, Physics, Computer Science, Biology, Zoology, etc.), all the basic health sciences like Anatomy, Biochemistry, Physiology, etc., plus Medicine, Dentistry, Nursing, Occupational Therapy, Physical Therapy, and Communicative Disorders.

WASHINGTON UNIVERSITY—ST. LOUIS MEDICAL LIBRARY

Access: Telnet
telnet://mcftcp.wustl.edu or telnet://128.252.152.1
At the PLEASE ENTER DESTINATION CODE prompt, type **CATALOG**
Once at the main catalog menu, you can search individual libraries or ALL
To exit press the telnet escape key

The following libraries have their collections listed in the Online Catalog of the Washington University Library and Biomedical Communications Center:
Washington University Medical Center Libraries:

- Washington University Medical Library
- Mallinckrodt Institute of Radiology Library
- St. Louis Children's Hospital Library
- Jewish Hospital Medical Library
- Jewish Hospital School of Nursing Library
- Barnes College Library

St. Louis Area Medical Center Libraries:

- Mary's Health Center Library
- St. John's Mercy Medical Center Library
- St. Louis College of Pharmacy Library.

WELCH MEDICAL LIBRARY GOPHER.

Access: Gopher
gopher:/welchlink.welch.jhu.edu:70/1

This is a medical gopher with a task-based organizational scheme. Topics include:

- Medical Library resources and services
- Basic science research resources

- Caring for patients
- Funding resources

Also points to other resources embedded in other Gopher servers

Contact: Karla Hahn
Internet Services Librarian
Welch Medical Library
Johns Hopkins University
KHAHN@WELCHLINK.WELCH.JHU.EDU

WRIGHT STATE UNIVERSITY FORDHAM HEALTH SCIENCES LIBRARY

Access: Telnet
telnet://130.108.120.22
When connected type **libnet** (must be lower case)
To exit select **h** (hangup) to log off

Catalog includes WSU's Dunbar Library (general library) as well as several hospital libraries in the Dayton area, including:

- Children's Medical Center Library
- Good Samaritan Hospital Library
- Grandview Medical Center Library
- Kettering College of Medical Arts
- Kettering Medical Center Library
- Miami Valley Hospital Library
- St. Elizabeth Medical Center Library
- Sycamore Medical Center Library
- Veteran's Administration Medical
- Center Library (Dayton)

NATIONAL HEALTH AGENCIES AND INSTITUTIONS

In these sections, the following abbreviations are used:

BIR, BITNET Institutional Representative
INFOREP, Local BITNET Support
TECHREP, local technical operations

FEDERAL

THE CENTERS FOR DISEASE CONTROL AND PREVENTION

Access: World Wide Web

http://www.cdc.gov/

In general, all information presented in these pages and all items available for download are for public use. However, you may encounter some pages that require a login password and id. If this is the case you may assume that information presented and items available for download therein are for your authorized access only and not for redistribution by you unless you are otherwise informed.

Contact:

NETINFO@CDC1.CDC.GOV

A complete list of CDC staff BITNET addresses is obtainable from:

HSPNET-L@ALBNYDH2 fileserver

CDC e-mail coordinator CDCJUK@EMUVM1

Also call Joan Kennedy at (404) 639-3396 for a directory.

CDC WONDER

Access: E-mail

WRH2@OPSIRM8.EM.CDC.GOV

This is not an automated e-mail server, so just ask for a user registration form for Wonder. Please be sure to include a U.S. Mail address.

Phone: (404) 332-4569 (You will be answered by Wonder User Support. Request registration material.)

FAX: (404) 488-7593 (Send a note asking for registration material. Please be sure to include a U.S. Mail address.)

The reason you cannot register automatically is the requirement for a physical signature to access some of the databases.

CDC WONDER is software for DOS-based microcomputers that creates a fast and efficient electronic link between CDC and public health practitioners. It is distributed free and uses a toll-free number to connect to the CDC in Atlanta. It was originally created to connect local, county, and state public health officials to national databases. It is now available to all public health practitioners. The data available through CDC WONDER come from the National Center for Health Statistics of the Centers for Disease Control and Prevention, the National Cancer Institute, the National Institute for Occupational Safety and Health, the Census Bureau, etc. Currently, CDC WONDER runs only on DOS-based machines. They plan to port CDC WONDER to other platforms shortly. There will also be Internet access sometime in 1995.

Contact: Dan Rosen
Public Health Information Systems Branch
Information Resources Management Office
Centers for Disease Control and Prevention
4770 Buford Highway
MS F-51
Atlanta, GA 30341-3724
DHR0@OPSIRM8.EM.CDC.GOV
Phone: (404) 488-7521
FAX: (404) 488-7593

DEPARTMENT OF HEALTH AND HUMAN SERVICES

Access: World Wide Web
http://www.os.dhhs.gov

The U.S. Department of Health and Human Services, Office Web server. This server provides a centralized directory of Internet-accessible services provided by the U.S. Department of Health and Human Services, including data from the National Institutes of Health, Food and Drug Administration, and Social Security Administration.

Contact: Tom Thompson
TTHOMPSO@OS.DHHS.GOV

FEDWORLD: NATIONAL TECHNICAL INFORMATION SERVICE

Access: Telnet, FTP, World Wide Web
The FedWorld telnet site now supports up to 50 simultaneous connections. Telnet to telnet://fedworld.gov or use the actual IP address of telnet://S192.239.92.201.

If all 50 connections are in use, you will be put onto a list to wait for the next available connection.
Please remember that all free files that are on the telnet site can be transferred using FTP from:
ftp://ftp.fedworld.gov (ftp://192.239.92.205)

Directories at the FTP site have the same names as the Libraries at the telnet site. Each FTP directory has a *<directory name>.LST* file that lists a description of each file in that directory. This list file is updated every morning.

White House documents available from the telnet site can now be searched using keywords assigned by artificial intelligence software at MIT. From the W-house Library of Files menu, select option **F** (find files) and then option **K** (search by keyword). Keywords tend to be very general: security, world and order, economy, health care, crime, state names, executive, act, etc. There is also an interface to most federal government databases, including:

* Navy Drug and Alcohol Abuse Prevention
* Human Nutrition Information Service
* Health & AIDS Information & Reports
* Indian Health Service BBS
* Nat. Institute of Dental Research
* Nat. Inst. of Health Grant Line BBS
* Naval Health Sci Edu &Training Command
* Medical & Health Services Information
* Disability & Rehab Data & Info
* Alcohol Abuse & Alcoholism Information
* Rehabilitation Services Administration

FedWorld also has a World Wide Web site that can be accessed using any of the common Web clients like Mosaic, Cello, and Lynx by pointing your client at: http://www.fedworld.gov

From the FedWorld home page, you can browse a list of more than 100 U.S. Government information servers, each sorted by NTIS Subject catagories. In addition, there is limited information on the services provided by NTIS, as well as access to many of the free files that are available from the dialup/telnet FedWorld interface.

The FedWorld home pages are being updated and improved on an almost daily basis, so if you aren't impressed yet, you will be later! We expect that depository library access to the NTIS Bibliographic Database Preview File to be first available from the FedWorld Web site. Access to the Preview File from the telnet/dialup site will follow in the very near future. While the public will be able to browse and search the abstracts in the Preview File for free, registered depository libraries will be able to select documents that were not available under Title 44.

Information on how to register will be posted to Govdoc-L in the future.

Contact: Bob Bunge
FedWorld Information Manager
BOB.BUNGE@FEDWORLD.GOV

FOOD AND DRUG ADMINISTRATION

Access: Telnet
telnet://150.148.8.48
Login **BBS**
Register as requested by the menus
To access it type **MANUAL** at the prompt and press <ENTER>. Then type
1. The manual will scroll down the screen.

This is the FEDERAL FOOD AND DRUG ADMINISTRATION's Internet link to its databases. The user will find reports and press releases on everything the FDA is responsible for. There is an on-line users manual.
BIR: Laurence Dusold
    LRD@FDACFSAN
    Phone: (202) 245-1413
INFOREP: Donna Kovalsky
    DBK@FDACFSAN
    Phone: (202) 472-5382
TECHREP: Laurence Dusold
    LRD@FDACFSAN
    Phone: (202) 245-1413

GENERAL ACCOUNTING OFFICE (GAO)

Access: FTP
ftp://ftp.cu.nih.gov

This site contains the Transition Reports released by the General Accounting Office on January 8, 1993, in the Anonymous FTP directory *GAO-RE-PORTS* at NIH (cu.nih.gov). They are intended to give the incoming congress and administration an overview of problems facing the nation.
ABSTRACT.FIL is a file with abstracts for each of the 28 reports
A-REPORT.LST is a file with the information below

TRANSITION REPORTS OF HEALTH RELATED ISSUES

- Health Care Reform. OCG-93-8TR. December 1992. 34 pp. (The file is *CG08T93.TXT* and contains 34841 bytes.)
- Health and Human Services Issues. OCG-93-20TR. December 1992. 33 pp. (The file is *CG20T93.TXT* and contains 36319 bytes.)

So that they can keep a count of report recipients and user reaction, please send an e-mail message to:

KH3@CU.NIH.GOV

and include, along with your e-mail address, the following information:

1. Your organization.
2. Your position/title and name (optional).
3. The title/report number of the above reports you have retrieved electronically or ordered by mail or phone.
4. Whether you have ever obtained a GAO report before.
5. If you copy a report onto another bulletin board, indicate which report and bulletin board.
6. Other GAO report subjects you would be interested in. GAO's reports cover a broad range of subjects such as major weapons systems, energy, financial institutions, and pollution control.
7. Any additional comments or suggestions.

GAO DAILY AND MONTHLY LISTING OF REPORTS

Access: To access both the GAO Daybook and Reports and Testimonies Issued in Month/Year:

Telnet CAP.GWU.ED

Login **guest**

Password **visitor**

Type **go gao** at the main menu

Ordering information is included in the GAO menu

The GAO now has available a daily electronic posting of released reports. The GAO Daybook is the daily listing of released GAO reports and the Reports and Testimonies Issued in Month/Year, includes abstracts of the items issued that month, arranged by subject.

Contact: Any questions or comments can be sent to:

Please do not use this address for ordering reports

GAO@CAP.GWU.EDU

NATIONAL INSTITUTES OF ENVIRONMENTAL HEALTH SCIENCE

BIR: Art Cullati
   CULLATI@NIEHS
   Phone: (919) 541-3432
INFOREP: James Dix
   DIX@NIEHS
   Phone: (919) 541-3221
TECHREP: Fred Castner
   KASTNER@NIEHS
   Phone: (919) 541-2552 (Research Triangle Park, NC)
National Institutes of Health
Bethesda, MD 20814
Roger Fajman, Postmaster for CU.NIH.GOV/NIHCU,

LIST.NIH.GOV/NIHLIST, NIH3PLUS

RAF@NIHCU
RAF@CU.NIH.GOV
Phone: (301) 402-4265
BIR: Joseph Naughton
JDN@NIHCU
Phone: (301) 496-5381
INFOREP: Roger Fajman
RAF@NIHCU
Phone: (301) 496-5181
TECHREP: Roger Fajman
RAF@NIHCU
Phone: (301) 496-5181

Further NIH nodes (for a complete list of BITNET, Internet, and DECNET nodes of their 3-Mail gateway, send a message to:
   SERVER@NIH3PLUS
   with a subject of NODES
This list includes some CDC, FDA, HHS, IHS, and PHS nodes (or contact Roger Fajman). The ones listed as NIH-only are also reachable as:
   USER%NODE@CU.NIH.GOV

NIAID

Contact:
Judy Murphy
Public Information Section
JM63A@NIH.GOV
Phone: (301) 496-5717
Deborah Katz
Office of Scientific Information and Reports

AIDS INFORMATION
DK30F@NIH.GOV
Phone: (301) 496-0545
You can also try calling the NLM Medline Help Desk at (301) 496-6095

NATIONAL INSTITUTES OF HEALTH

Access: World Wide Web
http://www.nih.gov/

The NIH WWW server of the Division of Computer Res. and Technology contains biomedical information generated or pertaining to the NIH campus. Most of the accessible items are already being processed by the NIH gopher server. More hypertext-specific items will be availble in the near future.

The home page has a color picture of the NIH campus. Hypertext links exist for the following:

- Biomedical-health issues and clinical protocols
- NIH Grants and Contracts
- Research opportunities at the NIH campus
- Molecular biology and modeling topics
- NIH computer and network resources
- NIH calendar
- NIH phone directory
- NIH Bethesda Campus info
- NIH Library
- Other NIH info services
- Access to other info servers
- About this WWW hypertext server

Contact: send comments about the WWW server to:
GOPHER@GOPHER.NIH.GOV

NATIONAL ARCHIVES AND
RECORDS ADMINISTRATION

Access: FTP

ftp://ftp.cu.nih.gov

The FTP directory can be accessed by anonymous FTP

Log on as an anonymous user; press <ENTER> (or enter your user name or **guest**) at password prompt.

The directory in which this information is stored is *NARA_ELECTRONIC* (**CD** *NARA_ELECTRONIC); it contains six files.*

Use the FTP **GET** command to retrieve copies of the files, as in **GET** *TITLE.LIST.DEC1793*

The Center for Electronic Records of the U.S. National Archives has updated the FTP-able file containing the Center's Title List: A Preliminary and Partial Listing of the Data Files in the National Archives and Records Administration *TITLE.LIST.DEC1793*

The Title List now has 12,273 80-character lines. Since last updated in September, entries for the following major series have been included: the 1980 Census of Population and Housing, STFs 1D, 3C, 3D, and 3F (Bureau of the Census); and the [Southeast Asia] Combat Area Casualties Current File, as of November 1993 (Office of the Secretary of Defense).

September's update included the following major series: the Institutional Investor Study, 1969–1971 (Securities and Exchange Commission), Bureau of Justice Statistics data files, National Medical Care Expenditure Surveys (Agency for Health Care Policy Research), and the Defense Wage Fixing data files, 1974–1991 (Office of the Secretary of Defense).

Contact: Theodore J. Hull

Archives Specialist, Archival Services Branch

Center for Electronic Records, National Archives & Records Admin.

Washington, DC 20408

Phone: (202) 501-5579

TIF@CU.NIH.GOV

TIF@NIHCU

Please send research mail to:

Reference Services

Center for Electronic Records

(NSXA)

The National Archives at College Park

8601 Adelphi Road

College Park, MD 20740-6001. Phone: (301) 713-6630

NATIONAL LIBRARY OF MEDICINE (NLM)

Contact: Robert Mehnert
Office of Public Information
RM94S@NIH.GOV
Phone: (301) 496-6308

Carolyn Tilley
MEDLARS Management Section
CT32@NIH.GOV
Phone: (301) 496-1076

Pamela A. Meredith
Head, Reference Section
National Library of Medicine
MEREDITH@LHC.NLM.NIH.GOV
Phone: (301) 496-6097

PUBLIC HEALTH SERVICE

Contact:
SURGEON.GEN@WHITEHOUSE.GOV

NONFEDERAL

AMERICAN MEDICAL INFORMATICS ASSOCIATION (AMIA)

AMIA@CAMIS.STANFORD.EDU
Phone: (301) 657-1291

HEALTH SCIENCES LIBRARY CONSORTIUM

Contact: Joseph Scorza
SCORZA@SHRSYS.HSLC.ORG
Phone: (215) 222-1532

HEALTH SPHERE OF AMERICA, INC

Contact: Jesse Asher
JESSEA@HOMECARE.COM
Phone: (901) 386-5061

HEALTH SCIENCES LIBRARIES CONSORTIUM

3600 Market St., Suite 550
Philadelphia, PA 19104

Contact: Joseph Scorza
SCORZA@SHRSYS.HSLC.ORG
Phone: (215) 222-1532

HEALTH SYSTEMS INTERNATIONAL

Contact: Richard Stevens
STEVENS@KOHALA.COM
Phone: (602) 297-9416,

SALK INSTITUTE

Contact:
BIR: Anne M. Quinn
QUINN@SALK
Phone: (619) 453-4100
INFOREP: Anne M. Quinn
TECHREP: Anne M. Quinn

STATE/PROVINCE—U.S.

ALABAMA

ALHELA

Access: E-mail
LISTSERV@UABDPO.BITNET
LISTSERV@UABDPO.DPO.UAB.EDU

The Alabama Health Libraries Association, Inc. (ALHeLA). The Discussion Group ALHELA is established to provide better health care for the citizens of Alabama as it is affected by the provision of health science information.

BLUE CROSS AND BLUE SHIELD OF ALABAMA HEALTH CARE INFORMATION RESOURCES

Access: Gopher
gopher://twinbrook.cis.uab.edu

This Gopher was designed to be a navigation tool for public medical information resources on the Internet. It was developed by the University of Alabama at Birmingham (UAB) Department of Computer and Information Sciences, through a grant from BlueCross BlueShield of Alabama for the express purpose of providing Internet access to medical information for all physicians and other health care providers in the state of Alabama.

Contact: R.L. Samuell
SAMUELL@CIS.UAB.EDU

ARIZONA

U. ARIZONA COLLEGE OF MEDICINE

Contact: Cynthia Tobias
Director, Office of Medical Computing
CLTOBIAS@ARIZRVAX.BITNET

ILLINOIS

STATE OF ILLINIOS SCHOOL OF MEDICINE

Springfield, IL 62794-9230
Terri Cameron, Automation Administrator
E-mail GH0225@SPRINGB
Phone: (217) 782-2419

UNIVERSITY OF CHICAGO MEDICAL SCHOOL (ROCKFORD, PEORIA, CHAMPAIGN/URBANA)

Contact: George Yanos, CIO
U08208@UICVM

New York

ALBANY SCHOOL OF PUBLIC HEALTH

Contact: Barry Krawchuk
BDK01@ALBNYDH2
Phone: (518) 473-1809

ALBERT EINSTEIN COLLEGE OF MEDICINE

Bronx, NY 10461
Robert Lummis
BOB@AECOM.YU.EDU
Phone: (212) 430-4211

BHRD-L

Access: E-mail
LISTSERV@ALBNYDH2

New York State Bureau of Health Resource Development.

COLUMBIA UNIVERSITY COLLEGE OF PHYSICIANS AND SURGEONS

Dept of Medicine: Reider Bornholdt
REIDER@CUCARD
Phone: (212) 305-3411
Health Science Campus:
Janie Weiss
SYSTEM@CUHSDA
Phone: (212) 305-7532

CORNELL UNIVERSITY MEDICAL COLLEGE

Contact: Nick Gimbrone
NJG@CORNELLA
Phone: (607) 255-3748

MEMORIAL SLOAN KETTERING CANCER CENTER

POSTMAST@MSKCC

MOUNT SINAI SCHOOL OF MEDICINE
POSTMAST@MSRCVX

NEW YORK STATE DEPARTMENT OF HEALTH
Contact: Barry Krawchuk
BDK01@ALBNYDH2
Phone: (518) 473-1809

NEW YORK UNIVERSITY MEDICAL CENTER, NYC
Contact: Ross Smith
SMITH@NYUMED

STATE UNIVERSITY OF NY HEALTH SCIENCE CENTER, BROOKLYN
BIR: Jack Lubowsky
INFOREP: Jack Lubowsky
TECHREP: Jack Lubowsky
LUBOWSKY@SNYBKSAC
Phone: (718) 270-3181

STATE UNIVERSITY OF NY AT SYRACUSE HEALTH SCIENCE CENTER
Contact: Jeannette Stiteler
STITELER@SNYSYRV1
Phone: (315) 473-5426

NORTH CAROLINA

SCHOOL OF MEDICINE
Chapel Hill, NC 27599-7045
Contact: Dr. Kirk Aune
Assoc. Dean Info Systems
KAUNE@MED.UNC.EDU

North Dakota

UNIVERSITY OF NORTH DAKOTA SCHOOL OF MEDICINE

501 N.Columbia Rd
Grand Forks, ND 58203

Contact: Don Larson, Coordinator Computer Services
UD165133@NDSUVM1
UD165133@VM1.NODAK.EDU

Ohio

MEDICAL COLLEGE OF OHIO

Contact: Jerry Levin
Assoc. Dean Academic Resources
LEVIN%OPUS@MCOIARC.BITNET
INFOREP: Karen E. Torok
Hospital Systems Coordinator,
TOROK%CUTTER@MCOIARC
Phone: (419) 381-5446

Pennsylvania

UNIVERSITY OF PENNSYLVANIA SCHOOL OF MEDICINE

Contact: Dr. Albert Shar, Chief Info Officer
SHAR@MSCF.UPENN.EDU
Phone: (215) 898-9754

MILTON HERSHEY MEDICAL CENTER

Contact: Alton Brantley, CIO
ALTON@CIT.HMC.PSU.EDU

UNIVERSITY OF PITTSBURGH MEDICAL CENTER

Contact: Sean McLinden, MD
SEAN@DSL.PITT.EDU
Phone: (412) 392-6800

TEXAS

MD ANDERSON CANCER CENTER

Contact: Richard Landkamer
MAILMNT@UTHVM1
Phone: (713) 792-6345

UNIVERSITY OF TEXAS HEALTH SCIENCE CENTER AT SAN ANTONIO

Contact: Conni Annabele
ANNABLE@THORIN.UTHSCSA.EDU

TRHEX (TEXAS RURAL HOSPITAL ELECTRONIC EXCHANGE)

Contact: John Oeffinger
CG8061@APPLELINK.APPLE.COM

UTAH

UNIVERSITY OF UTAH SCHOOL OF MEDICINE

Contact: Clay Epstein, Dir. Medical School Computer Center
CLAY@MSSCC.MED.UTAH.EDU

WISCONSIN

STATE LAB OF HYGIENE

Epidemiology, environment, etc.

Contact: Jim Leinweber
JIML@SLH.WISC.EDU
Phone: (608) 262-0736

INTERNATIONAL HEALTH AGENCIES AND INSTITUTIONS

ARGENTINA

HEALTH INSTITUTIONS IN ARGENTINA

Access: E-mail
If you want to reach all these institutes at the same time, send a single message to: SALUD@OPSARG.SID.AR
If you have any questions send a message to INFO@PCCP.COM.AR

In Spanish. 113 nodes.
A complete list of Internet nodes for institutions, hospitals, medical schools, sections of the Ministry of Health, etc. is obtainable from Marcela Guissana MD.

Contact:
Server and postmaster's names (in message to server put **HELP**)

Contact: Fernando Lopez
GUERRA LISTSERV@OPSARG.ALD.AR in body of message (opsarg=a for PAHO office in Buenos Aires).
Dr. Adolfo Galanternik
LISTSERV@DACFYB.SLD.AR in body of message (dacfyb= for DEPT. of Clinical Analysis at Buenos Aires Univ.)
Drs. Marcela Giussani & Alberto Barengols
SERVER@GUTI.SLD.GOV.AR on Subject line (guti=Hospital de Ninos, Buenos Aires)

AUSTRALIA

AUSTRALIAN ACADEMIC AND RESEARCH NETWORK AGENCY (AARNet)

GIH900@CSC.ANU.OZ.AU
Phone: + +62 493385

CANADA

DEPT. OF HEALTH AND WELFARE

Contact: Steve Scantlebury
STEVES@HPB.HWC.CA
Phone: (613) 954-6449

EMERGENCY PREPAREDNESS INFORMATION EXCHANGE BBS (EPIX)

Contact: Richard Smith
SMITH@WHISTLER.SFU.CA
Phone: (604) 291-4921

ONTARIO CANCER INSTITUTE, TORONTO, CANADA

Contact: Norman Housley
NETADMIN@UTORONTO
Phone: (416) 978-4967

ONTARIO MINISTRY OF HEALTH

Contact: Peter Renzland
PETER@ONTMOH.UUCP and RENZLAND@MOH.GOV.ON.CA
Phone: (416) 323-1300

CROATIA

CROMED-L

Access: E-mail
LISTSERV@AEARN

Croatian Medical discussion list. The intention of this e-conference is to inform an international community on current events in Croatia, particularly in the sphere of medicine. The intention is also to establish e-mail as a tool for easier organization of gathering medical and humanitarian help.

Contact:
Ministry of Health
Republic of Croatia
   Office for Cooperation between World Health Organization and the Republic of Croatia
   8. maja 42, 41000 YU-Zagreb
   Phone: ++38 41 430 621
   FAX: ++38 41 431 067
   WHOCRO@UNI-ZG.AC.MAIL.YU

EGYPT

WHO EGYPT (ALEXANDRIA)

Contact:
SYSTEM@WHO.EG OR
WHO@EGFRCUVX.BITNET
Khaled A. Hadi
MONDO@EGFRCUVX.BITNET

FRANCE

INSTITUT PASTEUR FONDATION (PARIS)

Contact: Gerrard Masson
GERARD@FRPSTR01
Phone: ++33 1 45 6880

FRENCH COMMUNICABLE DISEASE NETWORK (INSERM)

Contact: Philippe Garnerin
GARNERIN@FRURBB51
Phone: ++33 1 43 25 9226

NAMIBIA

KATATURA STATE HOSPITAL, WINDHOEK, NAMIBIA

Contact: Dr. Eberhard Lisse
SPEL@HIPPO.RU.AC.ZA

RUSSIA

CENTER FOR EMERGENCY MEDICINE, MOSCOW

Contact: Ilya V. Zakharov
ZAKH@HOME.VEGA.MSK.SU

WORLD HEALTH AGENCIES

INTERNATIONAL RED CROSS, SWITZERLAND

Contact:
POSTMASTER@VERW.SWITCH.CH

MEDICINS SANS FRONTIERS, FRANCE

Contact: Dr. JF Vibert
VIBERT@FRSIM51.BITNET
Phone: ++33 1 40 21 2929
FAX: ++33 1 48 06 6868

WORLD HEALTH ORGANIZATION, GENEVA HEADQUARTERS

Contact: Mr. Shunichi AKAZAWA
Network Manager
MANAGER@WHO.CH
Mr. David BERG
Director Info Technology Office
BERG@WHO.CH
Mr. Jim Duppenthaler
Dissemination of Health Statistics

DUPPENTHALER@WHO.CH
Dr. K. Hata
Info Manager, Tropical Diseases Research (TDR)
HATA@WHO.CH
Mr. Mark Wallace
Info Technology, Global Programme on AIDS
WALLACE@WHO.CH

WHO BBS MASTER

Access: E-mail, Telnet

You can get an account on the BBS by mailing the following information: Name, Address, e-mail address, terminal type (vt100, etc) and a short description of professional activities, to: BBSMASTER@WHO.CH

In July 1993, the Division for Health Situation and Trend Assessment (HST) of the World Health Organization organized a Consultation on Health Futures. As one of the follow-up actions to that consultation, an Internet Bulletin Board System (BBS) was created and is intended to be used as a permanent meeting place for a Network of people interested in Health Futures. The topics of the boards are currently:

- Macro Environment of Health
- Future Health Status
- Future Health Resources
- Emerging Health Technology
- Alternative Care Systems
- Tools for Health Future Research

The BBS has mailboxes, boards, a chat (IRC) area, and an attached file transfer facility. Postings and mail can be forwarded to any Internet e-mail address. The present BBS is limited to 725 registered users and is focusing on above topics, however; there is a growing demand for this type of communication and it is expected that a much broader BBS will be put into service at the WHO.

WHO GOPHER

Access: Gopher, Telnet
gopher://gopher.who.ch:70/1

telnet://gopher.who.ch
Login **gopher**

World Health Organization topics.

Contact:
WHO Internet Gopher Root Server Administrator
Information Technology Office (ITO)
World Health Organization (WHO) Headquarters
CH-1211 Geneva 27
Switzerland
Phone: ++41 22 791 2434
FAX: ++41 22 791 0746
GOPHER@WHO.CH
AKAZAWA@WHO.CH

WORLD HEALTH ORGANIZATION, REGIONAL OFFICE FOR THE PAN-AMERICAN HEALTH ORGANIZATION (PAHO/HEADQUARTERS)

Contact: Dr. Carlos Gamboa
GAMBOACA@PAHOHQ.BITNET

WHONCD-L (WORLD HEALTH ORGANIZATION COLLABORATING CENTERS ON NONCOMMUNICABLE DISEASES DISCUSSION GROUP)

Access: E-mail
LISTSERV@DB2.NLM.NIH.GOV

The Division of Health and Development of the Pan American Health Organization (PAHO) is pleased to announce to all participants at WHO Collaborating Centers on Non Communicable Diseases that the discussion group list WHONCD-L has been deployed at db2.nlm.nih.gov server as a part of the recommendation of the meeting.

Owner: Dr. Carlos A. Gamboa
GAMBOA@NLM.NIH.GOV

MEDICAL SCHOOL AND HOSPITAL GOPHERS

Gopher servers began appearing in institutions of higher education in the late 1980s. They quickly became a popular method of disseminating institutional information concerning curriculum, job openings, and current research. Most also carry institutional phone books, providing faculty and staff phone numbers and e-mail addresses. All addresses listed are in URL format. If you are using a Gopher client (Gopher software on your PC) use the information after "gopher://" as the address.

MEDICAL SCHOOL GOPHERS

Albert Einstein College of Medicine
gopher://gopher.aecom.yu.edu:70/11/

Australian National University John Curtin School of Medical Research
gopher://jcsmr.anu.edu.au:70/1

Baylor College of Medicine BioGopher
gopher://mbcr.bcm.tmc.edu:70/1

Baylor University, College of Medicine
gopher://gopher.bcm.tmc.edu:70/1

Bowman Gray School of Medicine
gopher://pandoras-box.bgsm.wfu.edu:70/1

Brown University School of Medicine and Program in Biology
gopher://gopher.brown.edu:70/11/brown/med%26bio

Case Western Reserve, School of Medicine—Biochemistry
gopher://biochemistry.cwru.edu:70/1

Cornell University Medical College
gopher://gopher.med.cornell.edu:70/1

Duke University Medical Center Gopher
gopher://mcissunp.mc.duke.edu:70/1

Harvard University Medical Gopher
gopher://gopher.med.harvard.edu:70/1

Harvard University School of Public Health
gopher://hsph.harvard.edu:70/1

Louisiana State University Medical Center New Orleans
gopher://gopher.lsumc.edu:70/1

Louisiana State University Medical Center Shreveport
gopher://gopher1.library.lsumc.edu:70/1

Marshall University Rural Health Care Gopher
gopher://ruralnet.mu.wvnet.edu:70/11/rural

Marshall University Schools of Medicine and Nursing
gopher://ruralnet.mu.wvnet.edu:70/11u%3A/musom

McMaster University Faculty of Health Sciences
gopher://fhs.csu.mcmaster.ca:70/1

Medical College of Georgia Gopher
gopher://gopher.mcg.edu:70/1

Medical University of South Carolina
gopher://gopher.musc.edu:70/1

NYU Medical Center, Hippocrates Project Gopher
gopher://mchip00.med.nyu.edu:70/1

SUNY Brooklyn Health Science Center
gopher://gopher1.medlib.hscbklyn.edu:70/1

SUNY Syracuse Health Science Center
gopher://micro.ec.hscsyr.edu:70/1

Southern Illinois University School of Medicine
gopher://gopher.som.siu.edu:70/1

Stanford University Medical Center Networking (SUMC Mednet)
gopher://mednet.stanford.edu:70/1

Stanford University, Medical Center
gopher://med-gopher.stanford.edu:70/1

Thomas Jefferson University Medicine Gopher
gopher://tjgopher.tju.edu:70/11/medical

University of California—San Francisco
gopher://itsa.ucsf.edu:70/1

University of Colorado Health Sciences Center

gopher://gopher.hsc.colorado.edu:70/1

University of Miami Biomedical Gopher
gopher://gopher.med.miami.edu:70/1

University of Michigan Health Sciences Network Information
gopher://thelonius.itn.med.umich.edu:70/1

University of Michigan, Medical Center
gopher://gopher.med.umich.edu:70/1

University of Mississippi Medical Center
gopher://gopher.umsmed.edu:70/1

University of Missouri Kansas City
gopher://gopher.med.umkc.edu:70/1

University of New Mexico Medical School
gopher://peterpan.unm.edu:70/1

University of North Dakota School of Medicine Gopher
gopher://gopher.med.und.nodak.edu:70/1

University of Texas Health Science Center San Antonio Gopher
gopher://gopher.uthscsa.edu:70/1

University of Texas Houston Health Science Center
gopher://gopher.uth.tmc.edu:70/1

University of Texas Houston Medical School
gopher://dean.med.uth.tmc.edu:70/1

University of Texas Houston School of Public Health
gopher://utsph.sph.uth.tmc.edu:70/1

University of Texas M. D. Anderson Cancer Center
gopher://utmdacc.uth.tmc.edu:70/1

University of Texas Medical Branch at Galveston
gopher://bluefin.utmb.edu:70/1

University of Texas Southwestern Medical Center
gopher://gopher.swmed.edu:70/1

University of Utah Medical Center Gopher
gopher://medstat.med.utah.edu:70/11/

University of Washington Pathology Department Gopher
gopher://larry.pathology.washington.edu:70/1

University of Wisconsin—Madison, School of Medicine
gopher://msd.medsch.wisc.edu:70/1

Virginia Commonwealth University Health Sciences Campus Gopher
gopher://ruby.vcu.edu:70/1

Washington University St. Louis Internal Medicine
gopher://telesphere.wustl.edu:70/1

Yale University Biomedical Gopher
gopher://info.med.yale.edu:70/1

HOSPITAL GOPHERS

Austin Hospital, Melbourne, Australia
gopher://gopher.austin.unimelb.edu.au:70/1

Beth Israel Hospital, Boston
gopher://gopher.bih.harvard.edu:70/1

Brigham and Women's Hospital (Harvard U) Gopher
gopher://bustoff.bwh.harvard.edu:70/1

Chedoke-McMaster Hospital (Canada) Gopher
gopher://darwin.cmh.mcmaster.ca:70/1

Massachusetts General Hospital/Harvard University
gopher://weeds.mgh.harvard.edu:70/1

Appendix A

Internet Software

The following list represents a growing trend in the development of GUIs, or point-and-click access to the Internet. Using this software with a SLIP or PPP dial-up account allows the user to access the World Wide Web's multimedia capabilities.

Internet Chameleon

Netmanage, Inc.
10725 North De Anza Blvd.
Cupertino, CA 95014
Phone: (800) 558-7656
E-mail: support@netmanage.com
System: Windows
Internet access provider: Netmanage, Inc.

Internet in a Box

Spry, Inc.
316 Occidental Ave. South, Suite 200
Seattle, WA 98104
Phone: (800) 557-9614 Ext. 39
E-mail: iboxinfo24@spry.com
System: Windows
Internet access provider: Generic

Internet Express

Phoenix Technologies Ltd.
Three First National Plaza, Suite 1616
Chicago, IL 60602
Phone: (800) 452-0120
E-mail: info@delphi.com
System: Windows
Internet access provider: Delphi

Internet Membership Kit

Ventana Media
P.O. Box 2468
Chapel Hill, NC 27515
Phone: (919) 942-0220
E-mail: sales@cerf.net
System: Windows
Internet access provider: CERFnet

Mosaic

National Center for Supercomputing
    Applications
The University of Illinois at
    Urbana/Champaign
E-mail: mosaic@ncsa.uiuc.edu
E-mail: mosaic-w@ncsa.uiuc.edu
    (for Windows-specific help.)
E-mail: mosaic-m@ncsa.uiuc.edu
    (for Mac-specific help.)
System: Windows; Macintosh System 7
Internet access provider: Generic

NetCruiser

NETCOM On-Line Communication
    Services, Inc.
3031 Tish Way

San Jose, CA 95128
Phone: (800) 501-8649
E-mail: info@netcom.com
System: Windows
Internet access provider: Netcom

Netscape Navigator

Netscape Communications Corporation,
650 Castro Street, Suite 500,
Mountain View, California, 94041.
Phone: (415) 254-1900
E-mail: info@netscape.com
ftp://ftp.mcom.com/netscape

System: Windows; Macintosh System 7
Internet access provider: Generic

The Pipeline

The Pipeline
150 Broadway, Suite # 1710
New York, NY 10038
Phone: (212) 267-3636
E-mail: info@pipeline.com
E-mail: info@psi.com
System: Windows; Macintosh System 7
Internet access provider: The Pipeline;
   PSINet

Appendix B

Internet Access Providers

The following list represents just a small fraction of the companies offering Internet access, both nationally and locally. National providers offer access through local "points of presence"; check with the provider to see if there is a number that will give you access via a local phone call. Local providers offer a variety of connection options, services and pricing plans.

A more complete directory of Internet access providers is the PDIAL, which can be obtained by sending e-mail to:

INFO-DELI-SERVER@PDIAL.COM

with the message **send pdial** in the subject line (leave the body of the message blank).

NATIONAL

Delphi Internet Services
Nationwide service
Phone: (800) 695-4005
E-mail: info@delphi.com

NETCOM On-Line Communication Services, Inc.
3031 Tisch Way
San Jose, CA 95145
Phone: (800) 353-6600
E-mail: info@netcom.com

PSINet
510 Huntmar Park Drive
Herndon, VA 22070
Phone: (800) PSI-0852
E-mail: info@psi.com

ALASKA

AK.NET
P.O. Box 92439
Anchorage, AK 99509
Phone: (907) 278-1787
E-mail: akitl@name1.ak.net

ALABAMA

Nuance Network Services
904 Bob Wallace Ave, Suite 119
Huntsville, AL 35801
Phone: (205) 533-4296
E-mail: info@nuance.com

Interquest, Inc.
799 James Record Rd, Suite A9
Huntsville, AL 35824
Phone: (205) 464-8280
E-mail: info@iquest.com

ARIZONA

Crossroads Communications
P.O. Box 30250
Mesa, AZ 85275
Phone: (602) 813-9040
E-mail: crossroads@xroads.com

Internet Direct of Utah, Inc.
1366 E. Thomas, Suite 210
Phoenix, AZ 85014
Phone: (602) 274-0100
E-mail: info@indirect.com

Primnet
2320 W. Peroia, Suite A103
Phoenix, AZ 85029
Phone: (602) 870-1010
E-mail: info@primenet.com

CALIFORNIA

Community ConneXion
2801 Cherry St, Suite 1
Berkeley, CA 94705
Phone: (510) 841-2014
E-mail: info@c2.org

HoloNet
46 Shattuck Square, Suite 11
Berkeley, CA 94704-1152
Phone: (510) 704-0160
E-mail: support@holonet.net

Sacramento Network Access
1765 Challenge Way, Suite 125
Sacramento, CA 95815
Phone: (916) 565-4500
E-mail: info@sna.com

Network Intensive
8001 Irvine Center Drive Suite 1130
Irvine, CA 92718
Phone: (800) 273-5600
E-mail: info@ni.net

EarthLink Network, Inc.
3771 Los Feliz Blvd. Suite 203
Los Angeles, CA 90039
Phone: (213) 644-9500
E-mail: info@earthlink.net

Beckemeyer Development
P.O. Box 21575
Oakland, CA 94620
Phone: (510) 530-9637
E-mail: info@bdt.com

The Network Link, Inc.
2817 Falvy Ave.
San Diego, CA 92111
Phone: (619) 278-5943
E-mail: stevef@tnl1.tnwl.com

CERFnet
P.O. Box 85608
San Diego, CA 92186-9784
Phone: (800) 876-2373
E-mail: sales@cerf.net

Institute for Global Communication
18 DeBoon St.
San Francisco, CA 94107
Phone: (415) 442-0220
E-mail: support@igc.apc.org

a2i Communications
1211 Park Ave. #202
San Jose, CA 95126-2924
Phone: (408) 293-8078
E-mail: support@rahul.net

QuakeNet
830 Wilmington Rd.
San Mateo, CA 94402
Phone: (415) 655-6607
E-mail: info@quake.net

LineS Communications
P.O. Box 150531
San Rafael, CA 94915
Phone: (415) 455-1650
E-mail: info@linex.com

Regional Alliance for Information
1525 Santa Barbara St.
Santa Barbara, CA 93101
Phone: (805) 967-7246
E-mail: rain@rain.org

Scruz-Net
903 Pacific Ave Suite 203A
Santa Cruz, CA 95060
Phone: (408) 457-5050
E-mail: info@scruz.net

The Well
1750 Bridgeway
Sausalito, CA 94965-1900
Phone: (415) 332-4335
E-mail: info@well.com

COLORADO

Internet Express
1155 Kelly Johnson Blvd. Drive
Colorado Springs, CO 80920
Phone: (800) 592-1240
E-mail: service@usa.net

Rocky Mountain Internet
2860 S. Circle Dr, Suite 2202
Colorado Springs, CO 80906
Phone: (800) 900-7644
E-mail: jimw@rmii.com

Colorado SuperNet
999 18th St. Suite 2640
Denver, CO 80202
Phone: (303) 296-8202
E-mail: info@csn.net

CONNECTICUT

Connix: The Connecticut Internet
6 Way Rd, Suite 33
Middlefield, CT 06455
Phone: (203) 349-7059
E-mail: office@connix.com

NetAxis
65 High Ridge Rd, Suite 363
Stanford, CT 06902
Phone: (203) 921-1544
E-mail: info@netaxis.com

DISTRICT OF COLUMBIA

National Internet Source
3220 North Street NW, #171
Washington, DC 20007
Phone: (201) 825-4600
E-mail: info@maple.nis.net

CAPCON Library Network
1320 19th St. NW Suite 400
Washington, DC 20036
Phone: (202) 331-5771
E-mail: info@capcon.net

DELAWARE

SSNet
1254 Lorewood Grove Rd.
Middletown, DE 19709
Phone: (302) 378-1386
E-mail: info@ssnet.com

FLORIDA

Florida Online
3815 N. US 1
Coco, FL 32926
Phone: (407) 635-8888
E-mail: jerry@digital.net

CyberGate, Inc.
662 S. Military Trail
Deerfield Beach, FL 33442
Phone: (305) 428-4283
E-mail: sales@gate.net

Gateway to the World, Inc.
9200 S. Dadeland Blvd, Suite 511
Miami, FL 33156
Phone: (305) 670-2930
E-mail: mjansen@gate.com

GEORGIA

MindSpring Enterprises, Inc.
430 10th St.
Atlanta, GA 30318
Phone: (404) 888-0725
E-mail: sales@mindspring.com

PING
400 Parimeter Center Terrace,
  Suite 155 North
Atlanta, GA 30346
Phone: (800) 746-4835
E-mail: info@ping.com

Intergate, Inc.
3600 Dallas Highway, Suite B4163
Marietta, GA 30064
Phone: (404) 429-9599
E-mail: info@intergate.net

HAWAII

Flex Information Network
1103 9th Ave, Suite 243
Honolulu, HI 96816
Phone: (808) 732-8849
E-mail: info@aloha.com

Hawaii Online
3016 Umi Street, Suite 201
Lihue, HI 96766
Phone: (808) 264-1880
E-mail: info@aloha.net

ILLINOIS

Ripco Communications
3163 N. Clyborn
Chicago, IL 60618
Phone: (312) 665-0065
E-mail: info@ripco.com

MCSNet
1300 W. Belmont, Suite 405
Chicago, IL 60657
Phone: (312) 248-8649
E-mail: info@mcs.net

NetILLINOIS
1840 Oak Ave.
Evanston, IL 60201
Phone: (708) 866-1825
E-mail: proll@illinois.net

InterAccess Company
3345 Commercial Ave.
Northbrook, IL 60062

Phone: (800) 967-1580
E-mail: info@interaccess.com

KANSAS

Databank
1473 Highway 40
Lawrence, KS 66044
Phone: (913) 842-8518
E-mail: info@databank.com

KENTUCKY

IgLou Internet Services
3315 Gilmore Industrial Blvd.
Louisville, KY 40213
Phone: (800) 436-4458
E-mail: info@iglou.com

MASSACHUSETTS

Internet Access Company
7 Railroad Ave, Suite G
Bedford, MA 01730
Phone: (617) 276-7200
E-mail: info@tiac.ne

Pioneer Global
811 Boylston St.
Boston, MA 02116
Phone: (617) 375-0100
E-mail: sales@pm.com

NearNet
150 Cambridge Park Dr.
Cambridge, MA 02140
Phone: (617) 873-8730
E-mail: nearnet-join@near.net

UltraNet Communications, Inc.
910 Boston Post Rd, Suite 220
Marlborough, MA 01752
Phone: (508) 229-8400
E-mail: info@ultranet.com

MARYLAND

Charm.Net
2228 E. Lombard
Baltimore, MD 21231
Phone: (410) 550-3900
E-mail: N/A

US Net, Inc.
3316 Kikenny St.
Silver Spring, MD 20904
Phone: (301) 572-5926
E-mail: info@us.net

MAINE

MaineStreet
208 Portland Rd.
Gray, ME 04309
Phone: (207) 657-5235
E-mail: cfm@maine.com

MICHIGAN

ICNet Innovative Concepts
2901 Hubbard
Ann Arbor, MI 48105
Phone: (313) 998-0090
E-mail: info@ic.net

MichNet
4251 Plymouth Rd.
Ann Arbor, MI 48105-2785
Phone: (313) 764-9430
E-mail: recruiting@merit.edu

CICnet
2901 Hubbard
Ann Arbor, MI 48105
Phone: (800) 947-4754
E-mail: info@cic.net

Innovative Data Services
22290 Green Hill Suite 42
Farmington hills, MI 48335
Phone: (810) 478-2950
E-mail: info@id.net

The Rabbit Network, Inc.
31511 Harper Ave.
St. Clair Shores, MI 48082
Phone: (800) 456-0095
E-mail: info@rabbit.net

MINNESOTA

Internet Connections
P.O. Box 205
Mankato, MN 56002-0205
Phone: (507) 625-7320
E-mail: info@ic.mankato.mn.uus

Minnesota Regional Network
511 11th Ave. South Box 212
Minneapolis, MN 55415
Phone: (612) 342-2570
E-mail: info@mr.net

MISSOURI

Inter
1505 Westport Rd.
Kansas , MO 64111
Phone: (816) 561-3688
E-mail: staff@inter.net

NEBRASKA

Internet Nebraska
1719 N. Kotner Suite B
Lincoln, NB 68505-5301
Phone: (402) 434-8680
E-mail: info@inetnebr.com

NORTH CAROLINA

Interpath
711 Hillsborough St.
Raleigh, NC 27605
Phone: (919) 890-6305
E-mail: info@interpath.net

NORTH DAKOTA

Red River Net
P.O. Box 388
Fargo, ND 58107
Phone: (701) 232-2227
E-mail: lien@rrnet.com

NEW HAMPSHIRE

MV Communications
P.O. Box 4963
Manchester, NH 03108-4963
Phone: (603) 429-2223
E-mail: info@mv.mv.com

The Destek Group, Inc.
21 Hinds Lane, Suite 23L
Pelham, NH 03076
Phone: (603) 635-3857
E-mail: info@destek.net

NEW JERSEY

Internet Online Services
294 St.
Hackensack, NJ 07601
Phone: (800) 928-1136
E-mail: info@ios.com

New Jersey Computer Connection
P.O. Box 6909
Lawrenceville, NJ 08648
Phone: (609) 896-2779
E-mail: info@pluto.njcc.com

Global Enterprises
3 Independence Way
Princeton, NJ 08540
Phone: (609) 897-7300
E-mail: market@jvnc.net

Planet Access Networks
55 Rt. 201 Suite E
Stanhope, NJ 07874
Phone: (201) 691-4704
E-mail: fred@planet.net

NEW MEXICO

New Mexico Technet, Inc.
4100 Osuna N.E, Suite 103
Albuquerque, NM 87109
Phone: (505) 345-6555
E-mail: granoff@technet.nm.org

NEW YORK

Long Island Information, Inc.
P.O. Box 151
Albertson, NY 11507
Phone: (516) 248-5318
E-mail: info@liii.com

Intercom Online
1412 Avenue M, Suite 2428
Brooklyn, NY 11230
Phone: (212) 714-7183
E-mail: info@intercom.com

New York Net
8204 218th St.
Hollis Hills, NY 11427
Phone: (718) 776-6811
E-mail: sales@new-york.net

The Pipeline
150 Broadway, Suite 1710
New York, NY 10038
Phone: (212) 267-3636
E-mail: staff@pipeline.com

Interport Communications Corp.
1133 Broadway
New York, NY 10010
Phone: (212) 989-1128
E-mail: info@interport.net

Echo Communications Group
97 Perry St, Suite 13
New York, NY 10014
Phone: (212) 255-3839
E-mail: horn@echonyc.com

ServiceTech Ink.
182 Moroe Ave.
Rochester, NY 14607
Phone: (716) 546-6908
E-mail: dam@cyber1.servtech.com

OHIO

APK Public Access UNI
19709 Mohican Ave.
Cleveland, OH 44119
Phone: (216) 481-9428
E-mail: support@wariat.org

InfiNet
274 Marconi Blvd, Suite 420
Columbus, OH 43215
Phone: (614) 268-9941
E-mail: sales@infinet.com

EriNet Online Communications
5551 Far Hills Ave.
Dayton, OH 45429
Phone: (513) 436-1700
E-mail: info@erinet.com

IACNet
P.O. Box 602
Hamilton, OH 45001-2
Phone: (513) 887-8877
E-mail: info@iac.net

OKLAHOMA

Internet Oklahoma
9500 Westgate, #120
Oklahoma , OK 73162
Phone: (918) 584-7222
E-mail: iconn@ionet.net

OREGON

Internetworks
P.O. Box 5127
Aloha, OR 97006
Phone: (503) 233-4774
E-mail: info@i.net

Free.i.net
P.O. Box 5127
Aloha, OR 97006
Phone: (503) 233-4774
E-mail: info-free@i.net

PENNSYLVANIA

FishNet
583 Shoemaker Rd, Suite 220
King of Prussia, PA 19406
Phone: (610) 337-9994
E-mail: info@pond.com

Telerama Public Access Internet
P.O. Box 60024
Pittsburgh, PA 15211
Phone: (412) 481-3505
E-mail: sysop@telerama.im.com

MicroServe Information Systems
222 Temperance Hill
Plymouth, PA 18651
Phone: (800) 380-4638
E-mail: info@microserve.com

RHODE ISLAND

InteleCom Data Systems
3 Franklin Rd.
East Greenwich, RI 02818
Phone: (800) 437-1680
E-mail: info@ids.net

SOUTH CAROLINA

South Carolina SuperNet, Inc.
1201 Main St. Suite 1980
Columbia, SC 29201
Phone: (803) 748-1207
E-mail: info@scsn.net

Sunbelt
P.O. Box 10630
Rock Hill, SC 29731
Phone: (803) 328-1500
E-mail: info@sunbelt.net

TENNESSEE

Telink
110 30th Ave. North
Nashville, TN 37203
Phone: (615) 321-9100
E-mail: sales@telalink.net

The Edge
P.O. Box 417
205 Research Park Dr.
Tullahoma, TN 37388
Phone: (615) 455-9915
E-mail: info@ede.net

TEXAS

Zilker Internet Park
1106 Clayton Lane, Suite 500W
Austin, TX 78723
Phone: (512) 206-3850
E-mail: support@zilker.net

MoonTower, Inc.
P.O. Box 4618
Austin, TX 78765
Phone: (512) 837-8670
E-mail: help@moontower.com

DFW Internet Services, Inc.
204 Belknap, Suite 200
Fort Worth, TX 76102
Phone: (817) 332-5116
E-mail: info@dfw.net

NeoSoft, Inc.
1770 St. James, Suite 500
Houston, TX 77056
Phone: (713) 968-5800
E-mail: info@neosoft.com

Internet Connect Services
202 W. Goodwin
Victoria, TX 77901
Phone: (512) 572-9987
E-mail: info@icsi.net

VIRGINIA

AlterNet
3110 Fairview Park Drive, Suite 570
Falls Church, VA 22042
Phone: (800) 488-6384
E-mail: info@uunet.uu.net

Capital Area Internet Services
6861 Elm St, Suite 3E
McLean, VA 22101-3830

Phone: (703) 448-4470
E-mail: info@cais.com

Global Connect, Inc.
497 Queens Creek Rd.
Williamsburg, VA 23185
Phone: (804) 229-4484
E-mail: info@gc.net

WASHINGTON

Internet On-Ramp, Inc.
E. 3724 11th
Spokane, WA 99202
Phone: (509) 927-7267
E-mail: info@on-ramp.ior.com

Northwest Nexus, Inc.
P.O. Box 40597
Bellevue, WA 98015-4597
Phone: (206) 455-3505
E-mail: info@nwnexus.wa.com

Network Access Services
P.O. Box 28085
Bellingham, WA 98338-0085
Phone: (206) 733-4523
E-mail: info@nas.com

Northwest Commlink
511B North Baker
Mount Vernon, WA 98273
Phone: (206) 336-3505
E-mail: glyacke@nwcl.net

Teleport, Inc.
319 S.W. Washington, Suite 803
Portland, WA 97204
Phone: (503) 223-4245
E-mail: support@teleport.com

SeaNet
701 5th Ave, Suite 6801
Seattle, WA 98104
Phone: (206) 628-0722
E-mail: igor@seanet.com

CyberSpace
300 Queen Anne Ave. N, #396
Seattle, WA 98109
Phone: (206) 281-5397
E-mail: sales@cyberspace.com

WISCONSIN

FullFeed Communications
359 Raven Lane
Madison, WI 53704-2488
Phone: (608) 246-4239
E-mail: info@fullfeed.com

MIX Communications
P.O. Box 17166
Milwaukee, WI 53217
Phone: (414) 351-1868
E-mail: sales@mixcom.com

Appendix C

Glossary of Mail Server Commands

The following is a comparison of mail server commands excerpted with permission from *Discussion Lists: Mail Server Commands,* prepared by James Milles, Head of Computer Services, St. Louis University Law Library, St. Louis, Missouri 63108, E-mail: millesjg@sluvca.slu.edu

To join a list:

Listproc:
SUBSCRIBE [listname] Firstname Lastname
(e.g. **SUBSCRIBE LAW-LIB John Doe**)

Listserv:
SUBSCRIBE [listname] Firstname Lastname
(e.g. **SUBSCRIBE INT-LAW John Doe**)

Mailbase:
JOIN [listname] Firstname Lastname
(e.g. **JOIN LAW-EUROPE John Doe**)

Mailserv:
SUBSCRIBE [listname] Firstname Lastname
(e.g. **SUBSCRIBE ENVIROLAW John Doe**)
Optionally, include the e-mail address at which you wish to receive listmail.
(e.g. **SUBSCRIBE [listname] Firstname Lastname [address]**)

Majordomo:
SUBSCRIBE [listname]
(e.g. **SUBSCRIBE ELAW-J**)
Optionally, include the e-mail address at which you wish to receive list mail.
(e.g. **SUBSCRIBE [listname] [address]**)

To leave a list:

Listproc:	**UNSUBSCRIBE [listname]**
Listserv:	**SIGNOFF [listname]** or **UNSUBSCRIBE [listname]**
Mailbase:	**LEAVE [listname]**
Mailserv:	**UNSUBSCRIBE [listname]** or **UNSUBSCRIBE [list name] [address]** (if you subscribed under a different e-mail address.)
Majordomo:	**UNSUBSCRIBE [listname]** or **UNSUBSCRIBE [list name] [address]** (if you subscribed under a different e-mail address.)

To receive the list in digest format (multiple messages compiled into a single mailing, usually daily or weekly):

Listproc:	**SET [listname] MAIL DIGEST**
Listserv:	**SET [listname] DIGEST**
Mailbase:	not supported.
Mailserv:	not supported.
Majordomo:	**SUBSCRIBE [listname]-DIGEST** (see below) in the same message, unsubscribe from the undigested version. (e.g. **UNSUBSCRIBE [listname]**)

Note: with those programs that support the digest option, whether or not to offer the digest format is within the discretion of the list owner; consequently not all lists offer digests.

To cancel digest format and receive the list as separate mailings:

Listproc:	**SET [listname] MAIL ACK**
Listserv:	**SET [listname] MAIL**
Mailbase:	not supported.
Mailserv:	not supported.
Majordomo:	**UNSUBSCRIBE [listname]-DIGEST** In the same message, subscribe to the undigested version. (e.g. **SUBSCRIBE [listname]**)

To suspend mail temporarily (without unsubscribing):

Listproc:	**SET [listname] MAIL POSTPONE**
Listserv:	**SET [listname] NOMAIL**
Mailbase:	**SUSPEND MAIL [listname]**

Mailserv: not supported.
Majordomo: not supported.

To resume receipt of messages:

Listproc: **SET [listname] MAIL ACK** or **SET [listname]MAIL NOACK** or **SET [listname] MAIL DIGEST**
Listserv: **SET [listname] MAIL** or **SET [listname] DIGEST**
Mailbase: **RESUME MAIL [listname]**
Mailserv: not supported.
Majordomo: not supported.

To receive copies of your own messages:

Listproc: **SET [listname] MAIL ACK**
Listserv: **SET [listname] REPRO**
      (To simply receive an automatic acknowledgement that your message has been sent to the list, use: **SET [listname] ACK**)
Mailbase: standard feature; you always receive your own messages.
Mailserv: same as mailbase.
Majordomo: same as mailbase.

To not receive copies of your own messages:

Listproc: **SET [listname] MAIL NOACK**
Listserv: **SET [listname] NOREPRO**
Mailbase: not supported.
Mailserv: not supported.
Majordomo: not supported.

To obtain a list of subscribers:

Listproc: **RECIPIENTS [listname]**
Listserv: **REVIEW [listname] F=MAIL**
      Can also be sorted by name or by country.
      (e.g. **REVIEW [listname] BY NAME F=MAIL** or: **REVIEW [listname] BY COUNTRY F=MAIL**)
Mailbase: **REVIEW [listname]**
Mailserv: **SEND/LIST [listname]**
Majordomo: **WHO [listname]**

To hide your address so that it does not appear on the list of subscribers:

Listproc: **SET [listname] CONCEAL YES**
                 To reverse this command, use: **SET [listname] CONCEAL NO)**

Listserv: **SET [listname] CONCEAL**
                 (To reverse this command, use: **SET [listname] NOCONCEAL)**

Mailbase: not supported.
Mailserv: not supported.
Majordomo: not supported.

To obtain a list of lists maintained by this mail server:

Listproc: **LISTS**
Listserv: **LISTS**
                 To obtain a list of all known Listserv lists, send the command: **LISTS GLOBAL**. To search for Listserv lists with a given keyword or character string in the description, send the command: **LISTS GLOBAL /[keyword]**.
                 (e.g. **LISTS GLOBAL /LAW**)

Mailbase: **LISTS**
Mailserv: **DIRECTORY/LIST**
Majordomo: **LISTS**

To obtain a listing of archive files for a particular list:

Listproc: **INDEX [listname]**
Listserv: **INDEX [listname]**
Mailbase: **INDEX [listname]**
Mailserv: **INDEX [listname]**
Majordomo: **INDEX [listname]**

To retrieve an archive file:

Listproc: **GET [listname] [filename]**
                 (e.g. **GET LAW-LIB feb94**)

Listserv: **GET [filename] [filetype] [listname] F=MAIL**
                 (e.g. **GET INT-LAW LOG9406 INT-LAW F=MAIL**)

Mailbase: **SEND [listname] [filename]**
                 (e.g. **SEND LAW-EUROPE 05-1994**)

Mailserv:	**SEND [listname] [filename]**
	(e.g. **SEND ENVIROLAW smith.txt**)
Majordomo:	**GET [listname] [filename]**
	(e.g. **GET ELAW-J BOYLE.TXT**)

The latest version of the entire document which gives a complete description of each type of mail server and how to use it is available by e-mail and by anonymous FTP as follows:

E-mail: send a message to LISTSERV@UBVM.cc.buffalo.edu. containing only the line: **GET MAILSER CMD NETTRAIN F=MAIL**

FTP: anonymous FTP to: ubvm.cc.buffalo.edu, **cd */nettrain*, get *mailser.cmd;* or**

anonymous FTP to: sluaxa.slu.edu, **cd */pub/millesjg*, get *mailser.cmd***

Bibliography

While the shelves of most bookstores seem overcrowded with Internet-related books, I have found a few that really stand out from the crowd.

The Internet Unleashed
Sams Publishing
1994
ISBN 0-672-30466-X
$44.95

Includes Windows disk with Netmanage software and one month connect time. This book is the creation of multiple authors, each an expert in a specific field. Throughout its 1,385 pages, the Internet is certainly unleashed. It is truly an intimidating work, but one that is easily digested. No matter where you stand in the novice-to-expert continuum, this anthology of the Internet was written for you.

The Online User's Encyclopedia: Bulletin Boards and Beyond
Aboba, Bernard
Addison-Wesley
1994
ISBN 0-201-622214-9
$34.95

Being somewhat of an on-line junkie, I found this book irresistible the moment I picked it up. While its primary subject is the Internet, as the title suggests, it goes far beyond it. In a remarkably simple and clear style, Aboba explains the complexities of networking, bulletin boards, telephone systems, and much more in a way even I could understand. A definite must for anyone wanting to get maximum use from their modem.

The Internet Guide for New Users
Dern, Daniel P.
McGraw-Hill
1993
ISBN 0-07-016511-4
$27.95

Written by the former editor of Internet World magazine, I think the title says it all. It takes the Internet to a reasonable depth for beginners.

The Internet Navigator, second edition
Gilster, Paul
John Wiley & Sons Inc
1994
ISBN 0-471-05260-4
$24.95

Revised and expanded edition of this excellent reference for dial-up users. It stands out as a very well written and designed text about the Internet and the background of the organizations that developed it.

Internet Instant Reference, second edition
Hoffman, Paul E.
Sybex
1995
ISBN 0-7821-1719-8
$12.99

After over five years exploring the Internet, I still fall back on this one for quick reference. It is a small book with simple explanations. Terminology is alphabetized and easy to locate.

The Internet Companion Plus: A Beginner's Start-Up Kit for Global Networking, second edition
LaQuey, Tracy
Addison-Wesley
1994
ISBN 0-201-40837-6
$19.95

Recommend for beginners and those who don't know where to begin; with a foreword by Vice-president Al Gore.

A collection of reviews of Internet books can be obtained by anonymous FTP from:

UBVM.CC.BUFFALO.EDU

Change directory to */nettrain*. The filenames are *nettrain.revs_1*, *nettrain.revs_2*, and *nettrain.revs_3*, etc.

They may also be obtained by sending a message to:

LISTSERV@UBVM.CC.BUFFALO.EDU

containing only these lines:

GET NETTRAIN REVS_1 NETTRAIN F=MAIL
GET NETTRAIN REVS_2 NETTRAIN F=MAIL
GET NETTRAIN REVS_3 NETTRAIN F=MAIL (author query)

More files will be added as time goes on. This archive is maintained by:

James Milles
Head of Computer Services
Saint Louis University Law Library
3700 Lindell Blvd
St Louis, MO 63108
millesjg@sluvca.slu.edu

Subject Index

Subject Index

INSTRUCTIONS FOR USING THE NETCRUISER SOFTWARE

System Requirements

To operate NetCruiser for Windows you'll need at least a 386 IBM-compatible system running MS-DOS 5.0 or greater and Microsoft Windows 3.1. You should have 4MB of RAM and at least 4MB of free hard disk space. You'll also need a 9600 baud or faster modem.

Installation

- Insert diskette into Drive A: or B:.
- From the Windows Program Manager File Menu, choose Run.
- Enter A:SETUP or B:SETUP as appropriate. In the "Welcome to NetCruiser" dialog box choose a directory for installation (default is C:\NETCOM). Wait for all files to be copied to your hard disk.
- Choose a modem type, baud rate and COM port in the dialog presented.
- Select a NETCOM telephone number closest to your location. After installation, you will have a new program group (NETCOM), which contains NetCruiser itself, NetCruiser Help, NetCruiser Registration, NetCruiser Getting Started Help and the NetCruiser Upgrade Program.

Registration

- Select NetCruiser Registration from the NETCOM program group.
- Click OK in the "Welcome to NetCruiser" dialog box. Fill in the "Registration Information" form. If a registration code is printed on your diskette label, be sure to enter the code at the prompt. If not, click CONTINUE on the Registration Code dialog box.
- Fill in the appropriate boxes for your modem to reach the NETCOM toll-free registration number, then click OK.
- If you are new to NETCOM select a user name and password. If you are an existing NETCOM customer use your existing NETCOM login ID and password.
- You will be asked to supply credit card information
- At completion you will be asked to select a local access number. New numbers may have been loaded into the directory during registration. The CHANGE INPUT button allows you to edit the information in the Registration Information form.

- **NetCruiser Help and NetCruiser Getting Started Help can be used without running the NetCruiser programs themselves.**
- **For 24-hour technical support, call 408 983 5970.**